Holy Covenant

Rebuilding the Families

Jami Sakely Vedenhaupt

Holy Covenant Rebuilding the Families

Copyright © 2013 by Jesus and Jami Ministry

P.O. Box 854

Hannibal, Mo. 63401-0854

Published 2013 by Jami Sakely Vedenhaupt

All rights reserved. No portion of this book may be reproduced, photocopied, stored, or transmitted in any form-except by prior approval of publisher.

Unless otherwise noted, all Scripture quotations are taken from the **New King James Version** of the Bible.

Jami's interpretive definitions are taken from Search EliYah.com: Strongs Concordance with Hebrew and Greek Lexicon. http//www. Eliyah.com/lexicon.html

Cover design by: Cynthia D. Johnson
@www.diverseskillcenter.com

Printed in the United States of America

ISBN: 13:978-1494455316 ISBN: 1494455315

TABLE OF CONTENTS

Acknowledgements

Forward

Introduction..................................1

The Shepherd 3

What is Covenant.......................11

Words of the Father......................23

A Little Revelation 33

It is not Good For Man To Dwell Alone.....45

How Does Man Live In Agreement with His Fellow Man................................55

Give Us This Day Our daily Bread..........67

Forgive Us Our Trespasses...................77

Surely Goodness............................87

Defining Honor............................97

His Kingdom Divided......................123

His Kingdom Is Peace..............................133

What About Grace...............................143

Part One: His Spirit Is Upon Us................153
Part Two: His Spirit Is Upon Us................161

Understanding Temptation.......................167

Holy Covenant

Rebuilding the Families

The storm that once held its grip is now powerless to keep its hold

Torrential rain is moving in

Flooding is apparent

Diversion has already been formed

This time no intrusion will be able to cross the threshold of this heart

This time there will be no breach

The barriers of God's Word have made every repair

This heart is in a place of rest with God

Acknowledgements

I wish to express my deepest appreciation to my family who still love each other in spite of our trials. Because all things work together for the good of those who love God and are called according to His purpose. I can praise God for everyone He placed in my path that unwarily has assisted me in the preparation of this book. Special thanks goes to my husband Lee Vedenhaupt and Minister Dixie M. Forte who patiently had to listen to me read paragraph after paragraph for over three years. Cynthia D. Johnson without her I didn't have a clue how to convert and set up my book for print and creating my wonderful book cover. May all glory go to God our Creator, His Son Jesus who is the Word of Truth, and His Holy Spirit that convicts all mankind of sin, righteousness, and judgment. Without these three we'd have no clue to what is truth.
Gratefully Yours, Jami Sakely Vedenhaupt

Forward

First of all I want to thank my wife and express my love and gratitude for over thirty years of her enduring love and patience. The Word of God says when a man finds a wife he finds a good thing. I truly believe I have found a good thing in Jami and our life together. I hope as you read this book and the Word of God that you will be enlightened. I have witnessed Jami through her time of studying God's word and many hours of prayer and sacrifice to bring this book into existence. I anticipate that this book will help you discover how to truly come back into Gods family. I hope this book will change your world forever. Her loving husband and companion, Everette L. Vedenhaupt

Introduction

Holy Covenant is a relational book of poetry and scriptural literature. I've set these words for our hearts in hopes of renewing our honor one to the other. Whether being a single individual family, a corporate church family, or the entire body of believers; we must give to each other what God has given us to rebuild what this present world has torn down **His Holy Written Words**.

Matthew 6:9-15 In this manner, therefore, pray: Our Father in heaven, Hallowed be Your name. Your kingdom come. Your will be done on earth as *it is* in heaven. Give us this day our daily bread. And forgive us our debts, as we forgive our debtors. And do not lead us into temptation, but deliver us from the evil one. For Yours is the kingdom and the power and the glory forever. Amen. For if you forgive men their trespasses, your heavenly Father will also forgive you. But if you do not forgive men their trespasses, neither will your Father forgive your trespasses.

Since the creation of man Gods plan of living at peace with Him and each other has had a total interruption. Because of this interruption one can hardly get through a day without trespassing against each other in some way. Therefore we will always have the need to forgive or be forgiven. We've all preferred doing things our own way. We need a Shepherd or guide to lead us back into the peace of Gods way of life.

We all like Sheep Have Gone Astray

Do you think you are all alone

Do you think you are the only one

All have gone too far

All have gone their own way

All will come face to face with themselves

Some are crying out

Some don't care

Decisions made without God

Left to one's self destruction always comes

Christ is the only way to reverse what we have become

Chapter One

The Shepherd

John 1:1

In the beginning was the Word, and the Word was with God, and the Word was God

John 1:14

And the Word became flesh and dwelt among us, and we beheld His glory, the glory as of the only begotten of the Father, full of grace and truth.

The Multitude

Mark 6:34 and Jesus, when He came out, saw a great multitude and was moved with compassion for them, because they were like sheep not having a shepherd. So He began to teach them many things.

Jesus was moved with compassion because He views us as sheep needing a shepherd. Sheep are defined as non assertive followers that need good leadership. Jesus knew our need to be educated in many things.

After hearing this particular piece of the Word of God I started reviewing my own learning process. I thought about how I've received my own Words of instruction from Jesus the Word of God.

First of all I realized no one learns all things in a moment.

Secondly, no one learns all things in one lesson.

Lastly each level of learning is followed by the next.

God desires us to always strive to gain more wisdom, knowledge, and understanding of His Holy Word.

I have heard different people say, that after they believed the Word of God and accepted Jesus as Lord and Savior, they can look back and recognize the different messages they know were sent to them from God. They've had people speak to them, sing to them, or hand them tracts, books, or bibles. God is always trying to teach us to recognize His voice.

Proverbs 9:5-6

Come eat of my bread and drink of the wine I have mixed, forsake foolishness and live, and go in the way of understanding.

The Father draws us to Jesus

Picture multitudes of people hearing Jesus is around and they just go as quickly as they can to see Him. He speaks and time slips away and they become hungry. Unaware of their surroundings, they've been led to a place without anything to sustain them. Jesus, aware of the need, won't let them depart until He has made sure they've had some nourishment to make the journey home.

Mark 6:35-37 when the day was now far spent, His disciples came to Him and said, this is a deserted place, and already the hour is late. Send them away, that they may go into the surrounding country and villages and buy themselves bread; for they have nothing to eat. But He answered and said to them, you give them something to eat. And they said to Him, Shall we go and buy two hundred denarii worth of bread and give them something to eat?

What did man have to do but follow the direction of Jesus to meet the need?

Mark 6:41-42 And when He had taken the five loaves and the two fish, He looked up to heaven, blessed and broke the loaves, and gave them to His disciples to set before them; and the two fish He divided among them all. So they all ate and were filled.

Jesus in this situation shows His power to take bread have His Father bless it, put it in the men's hands and see it multiply.

The Bread of Life

John 6:33 For the bread of God is He who comes down from heaven and gives life to the world.

John 6:43-51 Jesus therefore answered and said to them, do not murmur among yourselves. No one can come to me unless the Father who sent me draws him; and I will raise him up at the last day. It is written in the prophets, and they shall all be taught by God. Therefore everyone who has heard and learned from the Father comes to Me. Not that anyone has seen the Father, except He who is from God; He has seen the Father. Most assuredly, I say to you, he who believes in Me has everlasting life. I am the bread of life. Your fathers ate the manna in the wilderness, and are dead. This is the bread which comes down from heaven that one may eat of it and not die. I am the living bread which came down from heaven. If anyone eats of this bread, he will live forever; and the bread that I shall give is my flesh, which I shall give for the life of the world.

To believe that Jesus is the bread of life comes as one is drawn by the Holy Spirit to hear and learn from God Himself. When I was seventeen I heard this scripture and it drew my heart to Jesus. In the book of Revelations John writes, He stands at the door and knocks waiting for whoever will let Him come in. Here John writes, all who come to believe in Jesus are fed with words from heaven.

John 6:54

Whoever eats my flesh and drinks my blood has eternal life and I will raise him up at the last day.

Only the Words of God Produce Life

We have been taught many things that don't agree with the Words of God.

I remember when I was a little girl. My family used to always call me this certain actress. To them I was dramatically acting everything out just like her.

Why? Because unwarily, what we gobble up with our minds is what we act like.

Mark 14:22 And as they were eating, Jesus took bread, blessed and broke it, and gave it to them and said, Take, eat; this is My body.

Not everything we eat can be trusted to produce life. Some foods may make one sick and even cause them to die. It's the same way with words. Some words can bring life or death to ones soul and spirit. **(Proverbs 18:21)**

Jesus was expressing that we must partake in the fullness of His ways. Just as food must be consumed for the body to survive Jesus who is the Word of God must be consumed for the spirit and soul to have everlasting life.

John 6:63 it is the Spirit who gives life; the flesh profits nothing. The words that I speak to you are spirit, and they are life.

Chapter 2

What is Covenant?

Genesis 17:2-4

And I will make My covenant between Me and you, and will multiply you exceedingly Then Abram fell on his face, and God talked with him, saying: As for Me, behold, My covenant is with you, and you shall be a father of many nations.

The Covenant Between God and Abraham

Genesis 17:7 And I will establish My covenant between Me and you and your descendants after you in their generations, for an everlasting covenant, to be God to you and your descendants after you.

Our Covenant with God

Galatians 3:29 And if you are Christ's, then you are Abraham's seed, and heirs according to the promise.

By believing that Jesus Christ is Lord and Savior we enter into a covenant with God. By being Christ's we are Abraham's seed and heirs according to the promise.

Holy: to be set apart, to be consecrated, to show oneself sacred or majestic, to be honored, or dedicated.

Covenant: alliance, treaty, between God and man, a fellowman, or a husband to a wife.

Holy covenant: is to be set apart to honor a sacred alliance between you, God, a fellow man, or a spouse.

All Have Made Covenants and Some Covenants Were not Approved by God

2 Corinthians 6:14 Do not be unequally yoked together with unbelievers. For what fellowship has righteousness with lawlessness? And what communion has light with darkness?

The Holy Marriage Covenant

Genesis 2:18 And the LORD God said, It is not good that man should be alone; I will make him a helper comparable to him.

Genesis 2: 24 Therefore a man shall leave his father and mother and be joined to his wife and they shall become one flesh.

Mark 10:7-9 For this reason a man shall leave his father and mother and be joined to his wife and the two shall become one flesh; so then they are no longer two, but one flesh. Therefore what God has joined together, let not man separate.

Hebrews 12:15

Looking carefully lest anyone fall short of the grace of God; lest any root of bitterness springing up cause trouble, and by this many become defiled

A Covenant Family

God has a perfect plan for families to intertwine and function. His plan consists of a loving nature for each member to serves the other and should be so conscience of each other's needs this is covenant. They should bear with one another's faults never expecting, demanding, or becoming upset when expectations are not fulfilled. **(1Corinthians 13:7)**

Broken Covenant

It's time that we wake up. We have strayed from God's ways with the ways of the world. We have followed ways that have produced broken lives. Ended covenant relationships have ultimately left us broken men, women, and children.
Broken families through broken covenant relationships affect all we come in contact with. We try over and over to form new lives of love, but without a covenant lock, even those relationships can fall apart into ruin. Covenant joins forever and never forsakes. Only following the way God has planned for mankind can bring the results we diligently are searching for. His ways are higher! **(Isaiah 55:9)**

Sad to say, there are families where a member just moves on and doesn't look back. Those broken in heart and spirit may just go off and forsake the others. We try to understand this reaction of forsaking all that they knew. Just because we don't believe we would ever take this action doesn't mean others won't make this choice.

2 Corinthians 2:7 so that, on the contrary, you ought rather to forgive and comfort him, lest perhaps such a one be swallowed

up with too much sorrow.

Paul was distressed that there are those who choose not to forgive and love. Sometimes as a Christian one considers them self a master who rules the kingdom and is allowed to judge when to forgive. If someone has repented from causing the family injury we must restore those who have repented with love to relieve their soul from grief before sorrow takes over. Jesus explained the master is not greater than the servant as he bowed Himself to wash the disciple's feet as a sign that we all must be cleansed and forgiven.

Remember God is our healer and it's His will for us to recover and have abundant life. Jesus knew what it was like to be despised and rejected full of sorrow and grief. **(1 John 5:14-16)**

Isaiah 53:4-5 Surely He has borne our grief and carried our sorrows; Yet we esteemed Him stricken, Smitten by God, and afflicted. But He was wounded for our transgressions, He was bruised for our iniquities; the chastisement for our peace was upon Him, and by His stripes we are healed.

Ephesians 4:31-32 Let all bitterness, wrath, anger, clamor, and evil speaking be put away from you, with all malice. And be kind to one another, tenderhearted, forgiving one another, even as God in Christ forgave you.

Proverbs 11:23

The desire of the righteous is only good, but the expectation of the wicked is wrath.

Expect: demand you get the thing you want; you perceive it is due to you

Accept: take something offered

Desire: wishes, hopes, requests something

The desire of those led by righteousness will ask God to remove their offenses and to help them forgive those who have offended them. **(Mark 11:22-26)**

We should not expect a situations outcome, but accept that God will work in us the things that please Him. **(Philippians 2:13)**

Expectation

As I was growing up I can remember different things that would occur and what it took to finally get enough courage to talk to my mother; then to hear her say, hurry up I'm getting ready to leave. I'd be so offended that I had to hurry, I'd just clam up. Of course, I'd lie and say, it's nothing, and let her leave not revealing what I'd been exposed to in life that day. Why, because I expected her to respond in a different way.

When conversations happen like that, we get used to not communicating with each other in intimate ways. Then our communication pattern changes course and we learn to act as if things don't matter.

Acceptance Works Righteousness

People are busy with their own agendas. Successful communication requires this particular attitude.

#1 if someone stops what they are doing and say, let's do this quickly, we shouldn't get offended.

#2 we must be grateful someone has paused long enough to recognize our need to communicate something.

#3 instead of clamming up we need to speak.

#4 if they consider the situation needs any attention they may change their plans to tend to the situation at hand.

#5 we need to understand expectation and stubbornness only allows wickedness to rule the situation.

He has set up the family to have a covenant relationship with Him and each other. Covenant watches out for and provides for the others needs it never demands its own way. The future will come whether we <u>expect</u> or <u>accept</u>.

Paul's Care for His Covenant Family

Acts 20:32 So now, brethren, I commend you to God and to the word of His grace, which is able to build you up and give you an inheritance among all those who are sanctified.

The Apostle Paul had been arrested and would no longer be able to oversee the church family he loved. He entrusts them to God and the message of his grace. He's trusts Gods Word is able to build up and provide an inheritance to those who are called His covenant brothers in Christ.

2 Corinthians 2:4 For out of much affliction and anguish of heart I wrote to you, with many tears, not that you should be

grieved, but that you might know the love which I have so abundantly for you.

John's Brotherly Covenant

Revelations 1:9 I, John, both your brother and companion in the tribulation and kingdom and patience of Jesus Christ, was on the island that is called Patmos for the word of God and for the testimony of Jesus Christ.

<u>Companion</u>: participant with others in anything, joint partner

The word companion is a key word in the kingdom of God. John knew he must encourage us by making Himself our fellow companion to stay locked into. The prophetic word God gave John in the book of Revelations has gone down through time to reach us as we walk through this life

This verse reminds me of the game Red Rover where two teams lock arms and call one of the opposing players over to try and break though the chain, to capture or be captured. We must become spirit <u>locked</u> to each other <u>as companions</u>, holding tight to each other and not let the enemy break through and separate us from Gods love and from each other. John went to the Island Patmos and his trials so we would be encouraged through our own tribulations. Let's truly be our bothers keeper with all prayer, perseverance, and diligence just like Jesus, Paul, and John.

Chapter 3

Words of the Father

Wake up! Wake up! It's three a.m. He's calling me again. I hear the gentle voice say, Wake up I have something to show you. See over there, she has wandered off again I must hurry over there before a wolf comes. Such a precious little lamb chasing after butterflies again. I wish she would realize the danger away from the fold. She is always following after birds or anything that seems to catch her attention. She never sees any danger until it pounces down upon her. I remember when I had just in the nick of time grabbed her with my staff before she went off a cliff in the fog. Three or four times we started off on a journey and I had to go back and find her because she slept too long. I told her listen for my voice when I call because it's time to move, but she tells herself I want to lie for just another minute, she wakes up and everyone's gone again. By the time I arrive to the rescue she's gotten dirty, hungry, and wounded from the tight places she has gotten caught in. Oh! She's such a mess and a lot of trouble, but she is so precious to me I must go find her every time.

Seeing Through the Eyes of the Father

Studying the word of God shows us His truth which causes us to see where we have gone wrong with Him and our relationships.

2 Corinthians 7:10-12 For godly sorrow produces repentance leading to salvation, not to be regretted; but the sorrow of the world produces death. For observe this very thing that you sorrowed in a godly manner: What diligence it produced in you, what clearing of yourselves, what indignation, what fear, what vehement desire, what zeal, what vindication! In all things you proved yourselves to be clear in this matter. Therefore, although I wrote to you, I did not do it for the sake of him who had done the wrong, nor for the sake of him who suffered wrong, but that our care for you in the sight of God might appear to you.

God is Observing our Individual Care for Each Other

John3:19 And this is the condemnation, that the light has come into the world, and men loved darkness rather than light, because their deeds were evil.

When truth comes by the light of Gods Word it causes one to feel sorrow concerning ungodly conduct. A godly sorrow results when we see the effect and damage that of an unholy decision has brought to ourselves and those around us. Godly sorrow is what causes one to cry out to God for those <u>affected</u> for forgiveness and restoration.

Job 42:10 And the LORD restored Job's losses when he prayed for his friends. Indeed the LORD gave Job twice as much as he had before. Then all his brothers, all his sisters, and all those

who had been his acquaintances before, came to him and ate food with him in his house; and they consoled him and comforted him for all the adversity that the LORD had brought upon him. Each one gave him a piece of silver and each a ring of gold.

Job loved God but hated evil. All those who spoke to Job didn't know Gods plans for Job. Yet they and their words were there in the mist of his trial. Job couldn't do anything, but listen to the views of His onlookers. Job knew his life before God. They could only assume this affliction was deserved by Job.

Just like Job, when we go through affliction in this life only God knows the heavenly scene behind the story. God, in time unveils the truth and the worth of a trial.

We like Job are stuck dealing with those who believe they are our appointed judges. Only after Job prayed for his friends did God turn away his captivity and restored unto him twice what he once had.

God's Word has all the knowledge we need to be rebuilt. We must gain His knowledge; for it is the hope that gives clear vision for our steps every day.

His Holy Word teaches us how to speak words of gentle kindness. It teaches us how to stand firm on words of correction. It gives grace to abound, endure, and hold firmly to the truth of His Words.

2 Corinthians 5:21

Now then, we are ambassadors for Christ, as though God were pleading through us: we implore you on Christ's behalf, be reconciled to God. For He made Him who knew no sin to be sin for us, that we might become the righteousness of God in Him.

We are Made in the Image and Likeness of God

God is pure love. It is evident that other things besides pure love have come forth out of us. It is the Word of God that works its way deep down into the heart that causes us to daily learn how to love more and more.

One might argue that there are those who don't read the Word of God and seem to be okay. We must realize that God's principles have been integrated into mankind by His written Word. Looking around us we see that some people have better actions than others. This is because their instructors in life taught Gods principles without His name behind the principle; which causes one to remove God out of His own equation. If His name is removed then mankind takes Gods credit. The truth is mans righteousness at its best is still corrupt and needs the Word of God to reflect His true image of good works. No one in themselves can project His perfect righteousness.

2 Timothy 3:16-17 All Scripture is given by inspiration of God, and is profitable for doctrine, for reproof, for correction, for instruction in righteousness, that the man of God may be complete, thoroughly equipped for every good work.

Looking back at our likeness of God in troubling situations; one only needs to examine what image has come forth in the past and what adjustments need to be made for the future. Then start working on those adjustments. By applying Gods new found principles, for example pray for those who despitefully use you or love your enemies. With the help of the Holy Spirit one can learn to love and pray for those who try to trouble one's soul. This is how we daily conform to the image of God.

We live in a world that is reversed from Gods ways. The world's corrupted principles are mixed with Gods principles; this is what our mind wrestle against in. We need the Holy Spirit and the Word of God which is the Bible to discern within ourselves what principles belong to our Holy God.

It's not what <u>comes at us</u> that corrupt us; it's the words <u>we allow to come out of us</u>. I'm saying here; some things that happen to a person maybe beyond their control. Sure corruption may try to enter the soul, but we are the ones who decide whether or not we will internalize it and choose to act that way also. God's image contains love, joy, peace, patience, gentleness, goodness, faithfulness, meekness, and temperance.

It takes constant contact with God to project His image. We can look into the mirror of His Word and walk away with His reflection. Without that reflection we look like us and not Him. **(2 Corinthians 3:18, James 1:23-25)**

We have different reflections that pass us by all day long. These reflections speak out things that try to control our image.

Here's just a few of those so called reflections you fill in the blanks.

Your boss lies to you and you want to…....

Your child ignores you and you want to…....

Your spouse doesn't keep their word and you want to……

There will always be disloyal situations we encounter, <u>but our image should always follow Jesus who did not revile others.</u>

This is why we must frequently go back to the Word of God to continue our transformation of the reflection of Him. In other words daily we need to have a transformation take place.

Romans 8:28-31 And we know that all things work together for good to those who love God, to those who are the called according to His purpose. For whom He foreknew, He also predestined to be conformed to the image of His Son, that He might be the firstborn among many brethren. Moreover whom He predestined, these He also called; whom He called, these He also justified; and whom He justified, these He also glorified. What then shall we say to these things? If God is for us, who can be against us?

We are justified because we have faith that He was offered up for our offenses. As we identify our offenses and confess them as sin we take on His righteousness. All things work together so we can <u>receive His justification</u> which <u>brings His righteousness.</u> His righteousness is what manifests His glory in one's life. Then in a right attitude of grace, mercy, and love; His righteousness can be shown to our fellowman.

Romans 4:25 who was delivered up because of our offenses, and was raised because of our justification.

Romans 5:1 Therefore, having been justified by faith, we have peace with God through our Lord Jesus Christ,"

Colossians 1:27 To them God willed to make known what are the riches of the glory of this mystery among the Gentiles: which is Christ in you, the hope of glory.

Realize glory always belongs to Him, because He worked the right attitude within us to be conformed to the image we express; His love and His glorious likeness.

Knowing He is for us persuades us to let nothing separate us from His love. It is that persuasion that draws us back to His Holy Word to get an accurate reflection of His image.

James1:19-25 So then, my beloved brethren, let every man be swift to hear, slow to speak, slow to wrath; for the wrath of man does not produce the righteousness of God. Therefore lay aside all filthiness and overflow of wickedness, and receive with meekness the implanted word, which is able to save your souls. But be doers of the word, and not hearers only, deceiving yourselves. For if anyone is a hearer of the word and not a doer, he is like a man observing his natural face in a mirror; But he who looks into the perfect law of liberty and continues in it, and is not a forgetful hearer but a doer of the work, this one will be blessed in what he does.

Thank God for His mercy and grace through the life of Jesus Christ our Lord and Savior.

We must learn that we can obtain Gods thoughts and ways through His written Words. Reading and meditating on the Word of God brings change to our words and deeds.

This is the renewing of our minds we have been so desperately looking for. It's not looking at <u>our reflection</u> that blesses us. It's seeing <u>Gods reflection</u> in us that blesses our souls.

2 Corinthians 3:18 But we all, with unveiled face, beholding as in a mirror the glory of the Lord, are being transformed into the same image from glory to glory, just as by the Spirit of the Lord.

That is what causes all those around us to be blessed with His glory and not ours. It is in that holy loving reflection that the family is built.

So when looking into His Word we must see ourselves being transformed into His image. We must exchange the unattractive for the glorious.

As we allow His Word to be rooted deep into our souls we will walk away changed forever.

Chapter 4

A Little Revelation

Trained up

I was brought up by parents who happen to be agitated and screamed a lot with very little self-control. I know this has been a struggle for many households. So I grew up and obtained the nature to also be a screamer. I longed to be a quieter gentler person.

Retrained

I have found the solution in the list fruit of the Spirit is gentleness and temperance. Gentleness is to be mild and calm while temperance is to have self control. I daily read the Bible. I don't just open the Bible and say, Ah! Ha! Poof! Here's my Word for the day. I tried picking just anything out of the Bible for my daily reading. After I started studying Gods Word from Matthew to Revelations I began to understand how the Word of God is Spirit, truth, and life with the power to create the nature of God in one's life. I realized just opening up the Bible and reading anything out of Gods order only confused me. When I committed myself to read the Bible's New Testament in the order it was written the Holy Spirit began to retrain me in the way I should go. **(John 14:26)**

Then I read the Bible's Old Testament in written order from Genesis to Malachi. This showed me the creation of man and His disobedience to God. How the people were partaking in all the ungodly customs of those around them forsaking God and His way. The Word explained how God is searching for faithfulness in men. He's seeking for those who would listen to His voice and be obedient to His instructions. I realized that He has always shown mercy towards His creation. He promised redemption to mankind through the Messiah. Repeatedly throughout the Old Testament the promise of Christ the Messiah was prophesied to come and deliver God's chosen people. The Messiah was given to us finally in the New Testament in the son of God Jesus Christ. Jesus came and showed us the Father nature in himself. Jesus said He must go back to the Father, but promised not to leave us comfortless that He'd send the Holy Spirit to be our teacher and guide.

His Word is transforming me and it also will transform you, because it is the light of the world. Now when I study I might for example read all of Romans or John. I enjoy looking at the structure the writers use in whole individual books and apply it to my life.

Hebrews 4:12-13

for the Word of God is living and powerful, and sharper than any two-edged sword, piercing even to the division of soul and spirit, and of joints and marrow, and is a discerner of the thoughts and intents of the heart. And there is no creature hidden from His sight, but all things are naked and open to the eyes of Him to whom we must give account

Training our Children

Sad to say sometimes we spend years without the knowledge it takes to be patiently gentle. I raised my children and now I have opportunity to spend time with my grand children. I've noticed sudden looks of resentment appear on their faces as I use certain tones and volumes. I've become more sensitive to resentment and how its effects one soul.

God knows our intentions good or otherwise. I know if I have gotten out of control and have raised my tone and volume and I have caused resentment I need to ask forgiveness for not being gentle, there's no excuse.

One day I felt I should try to explain what resentment was and its effects to one of my grand children. I explained how we get words in our head that are not from God. These words tell us to get mad. I said did you know God knows what we are thinking? Our job is to look and see what kind of thoughts are trying to get in our heads. We can have good or bad thoughts come into our heads, but we should not ever like bad thoughts. We need to ask Jesus to take those bad thoughts away. I said if we choose to stay mad and not forgive someone, God calls that sin. When I get mad I don't like how I feel, do you? I have to forgive someone and stop being mad at them if I want to feel better. Then I think in my head, do I want to be mad or do I want to love them. I told them that Jesus loves us and forgives us. He came and died to forgive our sins. When someone is doing something wrong like yelling we should always pray that Gods helps us to forgive them. It's always good to ask God to help people do better. So we need to try to not stay mad at people, but forgive them and pray. Okay?

Retraining a Grown Child

A woman was telling me how she was angry with her father and wasn't talking to him. They'd had a fight because her father stole something from her child. She couldn't see how he could treat his grandchild like that. She said, she remembered what a terrible father he was. I told her, she must forgive and get rid of that bitterness toward him. She said, She was going to stay angry for awhile because she had the right to I said, Jesus took all our rights to hold on to bitterness. When He died on the cross; He carried to the cross bitterness and didn't complain. He was hushed within Himself so we can be silent toward bitterness. We have no rights to anger and deciding not to forgive others. Jesus said we must forgive if we want to be forgiven. He knew people sometimes just don't see what they are really doing to the hearts of others. You must try to understand your father doesn't see clearly. Jesus on the cross said Father forgive them they don't know what they are doing?

Not being able to forgive someone will cause one to burn inside with anger. Holding onto anger burns away our peace and as a result it destroys our joy. We must forgive others and receive His forgiveness to be full of Gods peace and joy.

When we allow ourselves to hold on to fear, resentment, or pain it causes us to want to control those around us. This behavior is not from the Spirit of God. His Spirit doesn't want to control others it causes us to truly love others and to self- discipline ourselves.
(2 Timothy 1:7)

1 John 5: 4-5

For whatever is born of God overcomes the world. And this is the victory that has overcome the world—our faith. Who is he who overcomes the world, but he who believes that Jesus is the Son of God

We Can Only Have One Thing in our Heart at a Time it Will Either be a Joy or a Sorrow

I want to take a moment to speak about hatred or hostility. Why because we are to be over comers of what this world has to offer apart from God. He who believes that Jesus is the Son of God overcomes the things of the world.

Ephesians 4: 22-24 that you put off, concerning your former conduct, the old man which grows corrupt according to the deceitful lusts, and be renewed in the spirit of your mind, and that you put on the new man which was created according to God, in true righteousness and holiness.

Put off the Old

We are instructed by the Word to put off the old man of the world and put on the new man created after Gods righteous and holy behavior.

When anger or hatred tries to manifest itself it is not of the nature of God it is of the old nature of the world around us. We are new creations in Christ this is the reason one must submit to God and resist ones fleshly desires.

We are to be over comers as Jesus was. Jesus sure could have given into Hate. There are many temptations that try to lead us to hate someone. Hatred, violence, bitterness, and such are of the old man. We can't give in to hostility, quarreling, jealousy, outbursts of anger, or selfish ambitions we must learn to resist their temptations. **(Galatians 5:19-21)**

Our Power to Resist Comes From God

James 4:7 Therefore submit to God. Resist the devil and he will flee from you.

When the things which are contrary to the Word of God rises up against us; we must immediately seek God and submit to His ways. In doing this we are resisting the devil who is trying to bring his mind to us through our thoughts. Note: These thoughts are not the mind of Christ. When sin tries to arise we must clean up our actions and get rid of impurities. If our hearts aren't broken by the Word of God sin will lead one away from God. Sins ultimate purpose is to separate us from God. As we present ourselves before God in submission to His mind He will elevate us to a higher way to follow. **(James 4:6-10)**

Jesus Taught us to Pray, Father Lead us not to Temptation, but Deliver us From Evil

Cain was warned by God that sin was trying to rule him. Cain's anger in the book of Genesis caused him to murder his brother Abel. **(Genesis 4:8)**

1. When someone has control of what we want or someone receives the payment we've been working to get hold of, a coveting hatred tries to occur within the heart.

2. When someone has the power to do good to his fellowman, but feel they have the right to do what they want at the cost of others, the person being mistreated could be tempted with hatred.

3. Power and rights are not reasons to sin against your brother's soul. Hatred is no excuse to exchange evil for evil. God says

that's a no no.

4. When we refuse to love our neighbor; we are teaching others around us its okay to hate.

5. The works of the flesh has been accepted as the natural response to most people. Some have been raised and trained by people who are blind to the truth of Gods Word. Looking around we see people everywhere doing such things and think it will be okay. Hatred and every other work of the flesh are just tricks of the enemy to steal our inheritance of Gods kingdom.

Galatians 5:21/b that those who practice such things will not inherit the kingdom of God.

Put on the New

Luke 6: 35-37 But love your enemies, do good, and lend, hoping for nothing in return; and your reward will be great, and you will be sons of the Most High. For He is kind to the unthankful and evil. Therefore be merciful, just as your Father also is merciful. Judge not, and you shall not be judged. Condemn not, and you shall not be condemned. Forgive, and you will be forgiven.

Do we love others? Do we even care if they will end up in hell? Once our eyes are open to the truth we are responsible to speak and rescue those within our reach. We must show God's love to those who refuse to love us for the sake of their soul.

I have come to this conclusion; I'm only capable of obtaining love for those who refuse to love me by my willingness to pray a blessing over their lives as they are trying to curse me. This is the only way I have found to rid myself of hells fire that tries to burn in my soul when offense tries to come. I choose Gods Holy Spirit and fire to set my heart a blaze with loving forgiveness. Yes I struggle with hatred at times, but love is the power that helps me to overcome it.

Let's keep on fighting the fight that says God's way is better. Then we'll all have the hope of not being ashamed that we didn't show love. He knows what true love for our neighbors will produce. **(Romans 5:5)**

Chapter 5

It Is Not Good For Man To Dwell Alone

The Good Thing

He who finds a wife finds a good thing, and obtains favor from the LORD. (Proverbs 18:22)

God said in reference to marriage, what He joins together do not separate or put asunder. **(Matthew 19:6)**

God has order and a plan, and man has his own plans. Do we want to deny self and do it Gods way is the question here.

We all have been worn for the worst by this sinful world. If you want out of a marriage you can always find someone to tell you its okay to quit.

There are going to be pop ups or sudden trials and temptations that will come to try our faith. Many people have not been able to get past some of these things.

1. What if your spouse had a misfortune and lost their attractiveness.

2. Would you marry someone you knew was going to lie, commit adultery, or do anything that would offend or injure your soul?

3. I've been married for over thirty years. I've gained a lot of weight and my husband who loves me says, would you marry someone you knew would eat too many ham sandwiches? I hope he's happy now he got me to add that to the book. All in all there are those who refuse to unconditionally love an excessively over weight person.

To Remain Committed with the Same Mind of Love is Covenant

I heard a testimony of a woman who had a sad life with many broken relationships out side of ever being married. She had lived with several men with no covenant relationship. Suddenly in her broken life she found Jesus and a God fearing man who wanted to marry her. She felt she needed to have herself tested for sexually transmitted diseases. She discovered she was H.I.V. positive and had to inform this man whom she truly loved of the shocking report. Now the man had predetermined in his heart they belonged to each other and still wanted to marry her. They had to make adjustments because of the sinful world's effect on their lives, but they nevertheless chose a Godly covenant between each other. This man married someone he knew was H.I.V. positive.

We all have been contaminated and need to be washed in love. Sin has infected all us. People have been damaged by the burns of life's fiery trials; in most cases it takes a miracle from God to be able to be handled again without feeling excruciating pain.

Ashes filled the weary heart

All looked blackened by the fire of trial after fiery trial

All was still as they lay there gasping for clean air to clear away the ash

The slightest cry remained as it rose to a holy place

A mountain top filled with love, mercy, and grace

The place where help comes from the cry was heard

Down came a gentle blow of holy spiriting air

It lifted away the ash as it left a golden voice of hope

It communed with a beautiful testimony of love

Fresh strength was the fuel that ignited the flame of truth

Lighting the way this heart should now go

God Says Marriage is Honorable

Hebrews 13:4 Marriage is honorable among all, and the bed undefiled; but fornicators and adulterers God will judge.

1 Corinthians 7:9 But if they cannot exercise self-control, let them marry. For it is better to marry than to burn with passion.

When society dictates to us one way and the Word of God speaks its holy truth in the other way; we must do as the Word says and not as the world does.

Today's society proves most people are not choosing marriage. Thank God He can bring us out of sexual impurity through marriage. If anyone has sinned they still can make it right and cleanse themselves before God and leave the rest behind. Remember God says He who finds a wife finds a good thing.

Love True Love

It was my reading of the book of Hosea that caused me to consider writing this book; **Holy Covenant Rebuilding the Families.** The book of Hosea in itself caused my heart to have a compassionate concern for my fellow man's restoration to a holy life.

God Instructs Hosea

Hosea 1:2 When the LORD began to speak by Hosea, the LORD said to Hosea: Go, take yourself a wife of harlotry and children of harlotry, for the land has committed great harlotry by departing from the LORD. (New King James Version)

Hosea 3:1 Then the LORD said to me, Go and get your wife again. Bring her back to you and love her, even though she loves adultery. For the LORD still loves Israel even though the people have turned to other gods, offering them choice gifts. (New Living Translation)

The book of Hosea has a direct correlation to Gods heart towards man. It shows the association to our covenant relationships and the strength of mind it takes to obey Gods personal orders to each of us to love our spouse. It illustrates the measure of God's judgments and forgiveness to provide us with strength to redeem them with our love. Hosea' obedience to God illustrates how we too can overcome this world's harlotry with Gods unfailing love.
We are to be as diligent as Hosea and retrieve our spouse in their hour of trial.

Proverbs 6:26 For by means of a harlot A man is reduced to a crust of bread; And an adulteress will prey upon his precious life.

This scripture states a man: the word a man in this reference could mean a man or woman is reduced by adultery. We must watch over each other and not let the adulterators prey on our spouse's precious life. Hosea had to go and retrieve his wife not allowing her to be stolen away through vain lust that would cause eternal damnation of the soul.

Here's a picture: Every time I see this one particular woman in public she always has to make a comment about some nearby man that she is lusting over. This is not uncommon among the people who are seeking to engage in harlotry. One day I spoke up and said did you know we are to be waiting for our own husband. That if

God hasn't chosen that man to be your husband you're lusting after someone else's husband. Do you want someone else to lust after your husband? I don't think she got it. That's when I walked away and prayed for God to give her understanding? We can't judge any one. All we are supposed to do is just try to explain Gods principles, walk away, and pray for their understanding.

Sure there are things in this world tries to overtake us, but a covenant relationship fights each other's battles. So when trials come to try and steal, kill, and destroy your marriage; remember what God has joined together let no man or woman put it asunder just stay committed to each other and the word of God.

Believe me there has been several things that tried to destroy my husband's and my love. I remember praying God put love back in my heart for my husband and I'm sure it was vice versa. Without the love of God being poured into our hearts there was just no way we could say we've been married for over thirty years.
(Romans 5:5)

God is the Healer of all Wounds.

This world has worn us all for the worse. We need to live new right where we find ourselves each day. Our deeds must reflect Christ by being faithful to our spouse or in some cases begin to be faithful. Love covers all sin, so when sin is covered by true godly love, then the pain of sin will also fall away by loves refusal to focus on the past. We must learn to serve each other as serving God in gentle kindness with healing words. God is Faithful to continually pour His love into our hearts for each other through the Holy Spirit. His Words of life are what will get us through the things that try to destroy our marriages.

1 Peter 3:7 In the same way, you husbands must give honor to your wives. Treat your wife with understanding as you live together. She may be weaker than you are, but she is your equal partner in God's gift of new life. Treat her as you should so your prayers will not be hindered. (New Living Translation)

By Gods grace men and women walk as co-heirs together, but the man should understand the woman is weaker. Both the husband and wife must have this same understanding that Satan wants to try and cause division in order to hinder their prayers. Understanding honor gives us the strength to act Gods way. I expect my husband to act a certain way towards me and vise versa but if one us should fail may mercy prevail. I hope we can be trusted to love and pray.

Honor: great respect, being trusted to act in a particular way

Love Sanctifies and Renews the Soul

A man needs to love his wife by guarding her heart and give peace for her soul. Unconditional love should be found within the marriage. (**Ephesians 5:22-31**)

Example: Sometimes I've had a disturbance in my soul and my husband might have chosen to...

1. The worst thing that can happen. He could take it personal and get offended then we both escalate into a greater disturbance.

2. He can ignore it by not recognizing I'm disturbed then my offense turns on him and my disturbance grows worse. Note: At this point I may choose to pray that he recognizes my disturbance and let God gain control of the situation.

3. He recognizes my soul is under attack and he drives away the disturbance by speaking words of peace and assurance then prays with me.

Respect Adorns the Heart

1 Peter 3:5-6 For in this manner, in former times, the holy women who trusted in God also adorned themselves, being submissive to their own husbands, as Sarah obeyed Abraham, calling him lord, whose daughters you are if you do good and are not afraid with any terror.

We are called to be co-heirs of God's promises. If a disturbance should occur with proper communication and understanding the husband and wife will work through it. Husbands and wives must build a relationship of mutual understanding and sympathy with each other and let love rule.

<u>Respect</u>: admiration, reverence, not to go against somebody

Sarah was called to walk beside Abraham as he followed where God was leading them. We as women need to have the same confidence in God that Sarah did by trusting their husbands' authority to lead them where God wants you both to go to fulfill the plans God has for you.

Trusting God allows the husband to love the wife and the wife to respect the husband. Love and respect allows them to enjoy the good thing God has blessed them with each other.

Communion

She closed her eyes with her head bowed

Waiting for his invitation

She so longs for his attention

She has so much to express

How long will she have to be self-contained

He bids her by his side

He takes his hand and lifts her face

He looks deep into his beloved's eyes

His queen-His bride

She's standing at his side

Completing the gap

Completing the life

Ready to commune with his wife

Chapter 6
How Does Man Live in Agreement with His Fellowman

The Load

The load was dropped soaking wet rock, dirt, clay, and sand

Just laying there in the hot beating sun hardening was inevitable

Turning the mass into fallow ground was the job lying ahead

It must quickly be spread and laid out for the transformation to begin

Digging, raking, separating then beaten into soft pliable soil would be the course of action

Laboring day after day

not letting hardness take it's petrifying grip

Most days just slightly watering was the supplement required to soften the clods into usable soil

Letting it move and spread out so gracefully ready to produce life

Just as a heart hardened by the rocks of offense that leave it overshadowed and useless

It must be transformed by the cultivating word of God

It has the power to dig, rake through, and separate offense and bitterness from fruitful affection

Letting it breathe and bring forth life

Explosions

There are situations that disrupt our lives and thus leave us in devastation. After there's been an explosion in life's circumstances and our hope bursts everywhere, don't just sweep it all away. Slow down, bend over or humble yourself before God in prayer and start to sort through the debris that must be sifted all the way through. This debris left untouched will have a hardening effect on our hearts. No one wants to tackle the job. It's over whelming, but once the heart becomes hard it is almost impossible to plant anything of value in it. We must not let the loads in this life clutter the purpose that God intends to bring forth for His Glory. We can't allow sin to take hold and weigh us down. Jesus is able to sift through and heal the wounds left in times of battle. He came to bind up the broken hearted and remove all the bruises from life's bump. Pray, He knows what will come forth beautiful and glorious from the war torn moments of this life.

Consider that things are always altered day by day. Every day we are reformed by life's situations. The potter doesn't recapture the old image. He has the power to form a new masterpiece of His own design. Hopefully we'll invite God's grace, love, and mercy to produce His best in us.

Hosea 10:12 Sow for yourselves righteousness; Reap in mercy; Break up your fallow ground, For it is time to seek the LORD, Till He comes and rains righteousness on you.

Letting Go of Any Heavy Load

Hebrews 12:1-3 Therefore we also, since we are surrounded by so great a cloud of witnesses, let us lay aside every weight, and the sin which so easily ensnares us, and let us run with endurance the race that is set before us, looking unto Jesus, the author and finisher of our faith, who for the joy that was set before Him endured the cross, despising the shame, and has sat down at the right hand of the throne of God. For consider Him who endured such hostility from sinners against Himself, lest you become weary and discouraged in your souls.

Jesus was pushed by hostile men right in the face with every temptation. He knew what it was to despise shame and let God handle things. He fought the battle so we can lay aside the weight of sin that would come to exhaust and discourage the soul.

If sin's temptation is not stripped off it will weigh one down and harden the soul. Consider Jesus and just let temptation go.

Hebrews 12: 14-15 Pursue peace with all people, and holiness, without which no one will see the Lord: looking carefully lest anyone fall short of the grace of God; lest any root of bitterness springing up cause trouble, and by this many become defiled;

Loving Our Neighbor

How do we walk in agreement with our fellow man? We need to keep pace with each other on this journey of time until God says, one of you goes this way and the other go that way. We are to walk in love with our fellow man daily and freely give to meet each others needs. It's our time, friendship, encouragement, instruction, finances, food, possessions, or anything that God has deposited into our lives we are to exchange with each other. At times it may seem difficult to stay in these relationships, The Apostle Paul traveled with Silas for awhile, and he also traveled with Barnabas, every minute in time spent together had significant purpose. Because of God's plans for us we just can't easily dismiss some of our relationships.

Love and Respect in General Relationships

God specifically connects us to our friends and the things we incur during the course of time. Everyone has their own struggles in dealing with their own ideas and feelings of superiority to other individuals as they try to fit in. When one's self-esteem becomes altered during any struggle, a feeling of rejection may occur. So out of an insecure, coveting, or jealous nature comments or gestures may arise behind each other's backs. In spite of this behavior we somehow love our friends enough to pretend it doesn't matter. Then the pretending it doesn't matter comes to a painful end. We all of a sudden just want to feel better and unexpected words just come popping out of our mouth in time of pain. Those around us begin being stung as the words flow out.

God Sends His Truth

How do we love in spite of the disaster? The gentle truth is, we want to feel better and have the ability to love someone to the fullest. To achieve this we must see Gods truth through His Holy Word of light. As we see truth and sin as it really is, then our minds can adjust to real enduring love.

God has His way of working truth into every situation to bring forth abundant life. Through God's love one is able to discover that cracking jokes at the expense of someone's soul does not bring forth abundant life in our relationships. As His Word of truth reveals the sin one must decide to act clean before God and stop theses gestures behind one another's backs. God truly knows all intent of the heart whether good or not. He's the discerner and divider of our soul and spirit. **(Hebrews 4:12)**

As we realize that God has been drawing us back into each other's company to heal us of all past offenses through His love being poured out to receive each other's forgiveness. Real life in Christ begins as we ourselves learn to love our neighbors as our self.

Romans 5:3-5 states that the glory of God is that our tribulations will produce perseverance then character then hope which doesn't disappoint us, because the love of God has been poured into our heart through His Holy Spirit that God gave to us.

That is exactly what He does, if we call upon Him. He knows the He has thoughts towards us of peace and not evil to give us a future and a hope. **(Jeremiah 29:11)**

Whether friends of choice, co-workers, or individuals of the church family; we need to care for the hearts we are in contact with.

This love is the love that penetrates through all things. The reality is this, that one's trials have stained and marred the image of God within us. When we see the joint weakness of all mankind, the need to overcome sin and become like Him, forgiveness becomes a natural preference. This light helps us to prefer each others needs before our own.

Man must not go by what he sees, but by the eye of what Gods sees, through the light of His Word.

<u>Unregenerate</u>: not reborn spiritually, not yielded, or stubborn

When we come to the knowledge of the depth of God's love for us in our unregenerate man then we can begin to look past the eye of circumstance, and the through the eye of transformation of man by the Word of God.

God's eye is ever upon us. He is God. We on the other hand are man. God is the Ancient of Days who is always seeing His creation as the apple of His eye. He sends help in time of trouble. His help is not always physical but, it always has care for the spiritual.

(The Ancient of Days) sounds mysterious huh? Well it fantastic! I get really excited to think of God as the Ancient of Days. Picture this, some thing comes up missing and no one knows what happened, we can only speculate. The Ancient of Days on the other hand knows, but how? Well He doesn't sleep, He doesn't ever come down from His judgment seat, He always is sitting and observing everything, and nothing ever slips by His view. With such precise discernment He takes it all in, in His perfect judgment and only responds in truth. That my friend is the Ancient of Days described in the book of Daniel, at the end of times, bringing all works into judgment.
(Psalms 121:4) (Daniel 7: 9, 13, 22) (Job 12:12)

<u>The Valley of the Shadow of Death</u>

I had someone say to me once, find out where Jesus was during your hour of brokenness. In the hour that ones soul has been sinned against to find out what Jesus was doing. To me that was the most ridiculous thing I ever heard. Find Jesus? How do you find Jesus when something bad has happened?

Where was God, was my question. If He watches over His people, where was He, was my real question.

We all have experienced transgressions darkness as it hits us Right Square in the face.

At the age of nine I experienced my first glimpse of darkness.

A childhood acquaintance had become shattered. Their little life was surrounded by a household of immorality. This darkness crept its way into my heart through their words. The family didn't have God's light to destroy sins darkness, so, it just slithered its way into their hearts. I never spoke to my parents about the things I was being told. Children do not know what to do when these situations arise. Why didn't I speak to my parents, is what I have tried to figure out.

These are some possible reasons
#1 fear
#2 hurry up I'm leaving
#3 your not to interrupts adults while they're talking
#4 not now I'm busy
#5 be quiet

My ultimate conclusion is this, It's hard for a child to find room to speak.

Dawns Breaking Light

Something wonderful and amazing also was spoken to me that year, the name Jesus.

Another little child invited me to go ride on a bus forty five minutes away to a church. Getting on that bus and entering that church was just so exciting to a nine year old. As the man at the church spoke I found my attention also drawn to his words. He talked about Jesus, and asked did anyone want to ask Jesus to forgive them of their sins, to spend an eternity with God in heaven. I got up and walked with what seemed a hundred people. We went to the front and I said a prayer to Jesus, and asked Him to come and live in my heart and forgive me for the wrong things I do. With some explanation I was asked did I want to be baptized. I said, yes. As we walked to get baptized the crowd of people split, men and boys went this way and women and girls went that way. Next I found myself in a huge dressing room with shelves of white gowns, bathing caps, and towels. Then one by one we all changed into these white gowns and bathing caps and lined up to get baptized. Then one at a time we went into the water to be baptized. I got back on the bus and back to my little world. I can't recall all my emotions then, but looking back on that time, even though I didn't realize it; Jesus had always been right there living inside of me.

Several years later I was working at a hotel as a desk clerk in a different state. A college choral group had stayed overnight in the hotel from that same church. Amazingly before they left they wanted to sing to me a song. The words in the song said, Jesus chariot was coming and was I ready for heaven. Some may call that coincidence, but I now know that God sent a little bus to me at age nine and He sent the second bus forty years later. Why, just because He loves me and wanted to confirm He's always been watching over me.

So the answer is this where was Jesus?

Where was God?

Where was the Holy Spirit?

All of them together came to me at the age of nine. Even though I accepted them into my life I still didn't know the fullness of this acceptance.

It has taken time for me to see the effects of both sets of words presented to my soul when I was nine. Sin and righteousness both had their effects, but I have found Jesus came to lead me to the path of righteousness. He came to seek and rescue the lost, <u>lost in this world's words of sin.</u> Jesus is the Word of God in Him we find true life. This present world is dark with sin, but His ever present light has come from heaven to this world to show us the way home to our Holy God. **(John 8:12)**

Psalms 17:8 Uphold my steps in your paths that my footsteps may not slip. I have called upon you, for you will hear me, O God; Incline your ear to me, and hear my speech. Show your marvelous loving-kindness by your right hand, O You who save those who trust in You From those who rise up against them. Keep me as the apple of your eye; Hide me under the shadow of your wings.

Hopes Uplifting Light

Darkness nothing is visible, no path, no direction

Where do I go, what should I do, why should I move

There's nothing I know. . . .

Silhouette's appearing through distorted vision

Light has reached through the darkness giving definition to everything that surrounds

The light is never ending always communing with life

A transcending of illumination that pierces asunder through to the deepest core

It seeks and reveals everything top through bottom

And all is exposed for the truth it reveals

There's a sudden meaning to path and direction

Chapter 7

Give us this day

Our daily bread

Psalms 18:6 in my distress I called upon the LORD, and cried out to my God; He heard my voice from His temple, and my cry came before Him, even to His ears.

Our cries must arise to God's ears. It seems so easy to cry to anyone we believe is listening. Only Gods wisdom brings life. Crying out and getting advice from those without His Words of life may only bring us tragedy.

Echoes

We have been given the ability by God to meditate on words.

Echoing words repeat themselves in our souls.

When someone speaks and it echoes over and over words like; I'd be mad too, I can't believe they did that to you, or are you going to put up with that? We have to ask our self, is this what the Word of God says?

What is Truth

For too long we have sought mans advice as our preference for answers not even considering Gods voice.

Man's voice has learned to agree with mankind's opinion of seeking justice. In having no tolerance and doing as others have done in similar situations there is no mercy or forgiveness following advice like that.

God's Word echoes truth to our inner most being, to love above all else.

No wonder we have been drowning in tears of self pity. We can groan all we want but, without crying out to God and searching His Word for our answers, we are just swimming in our own tears. No man can ever take God's place when it comes to resolution. We need things resolved and not stirred up by man's own destruction. Sure there are those men and women of God who have Godly wisdom, but be sure they are sound when it comes to speaking truth. Just because someone goes to church doesn't mean they are giving out Godly advice.

If the advice doesn't say exactly what the Word of God says it's not the Word of God. It's heresy and foul and will bring damage and darkness to your life. Confusion will arise and it won't be clear to see the direction you need to go.

Our we Playing by the Rules

2 Timothy 2:5 And also if anyone competes in athletics, he is not crowned unless he competes according to the rules.

(Our problem) has lied in that we haven't allowed the Word of life to be in control of our lives.

(Our solution) is to rightly divide the word of truth, which can only be accomplished by studying it. We cannot obtain His blessing without doing it His way.

Psalms 119:105 Your word *is* a lamp to my feet and a light to my path.

His Word is Our Daily Bread

Matthew 3:1-3 in those days John the Baptist came preaching in the wilderness of Judea, and saying, Repent, for the kingdom of heaven is at hand! For this is he who was spoken of by the prophet Isaiah, saying: The voice of one crying in the wilderness: Prepare the way of the LORD; Make His paths straight.

Matthew 4:17 From that time Jesus began to preach and to say, "Repent, for the kingdom of heaven is at hand

The message was (Repent, for the kingdom of heaven is at hand). This message says; don't live like the other nations or people that have forsaken Gods holy ways to follow after our own heart's sin. Live like you're in the Kingdom of heaven now. We must become like John and Jesus announce the coming of the return of Christ for those before us who don't know the Word of God. Saying, prepare and get yourself clean and ready before your Holy God without delay. **(John 14:3)**

The truth is, not all will choose Christ. Some of the people we love will choose the dark path away from God. They'll focus on wickedness and darkness. They won't confess that they are sinners. They won't take the path to eternal life. In light of this truth on our watch for the souls around us we must still ask God for their salvation through our prayers. **(1 John 5:16) (Revelations 8:4)**

Only God knows who will accept or reject eternal life. Jesus is faithful and true and God is not slow in His promise to us to bring us to Him. His wish is that no one should perish. **(2 Peter 3:9)**

John 17:17 Sanctify them by Your truth. Your word is truth.

God so loved the world that He gave His only Son Jesus. To those who believe in Him He will give life. He came to show us the way to God. **(John 3:16)**

When God raised Jesus from the dead, He raised Him far above the things that control this world to a heavenly kingdom of authority. Jesus was afflicted for us and **through His overcoming victory He fought and won our battles for us.** When we received Jesus as Lord and Savior, we were raised together with Him above the afflictions that try this present world. In receiving His Spirit we have been sealed as the possession of God until we enter heaven for all eternity. The Holy Spirit is our guarantee that brings us the inheritance to share in all that He has by becoming His children. **(Ephesians 2:6) (Ephesians 1:13-23)**

1 Corinthians 13:7 says that love bears, believes, hopes, and endures all things.

Bear: cover or protect

Believe: have trust

Hope: wait for

Endure: hold fast, trust, wait during trials

It is not for us to know who will accept Jesus. It is for us to act like God in loving others.

Reflections of truth

Risen above principalities, power and might

Transformed into the image of Christ

Free from guilt, shame, and pain

Christ has set the law of love in our life

Glancing at those from the past by Gods revealing light

Saddened, by those without knowledge

Unknowingly caught in sins blinding cycle not having Christ

Wretched without internal peace not having loves light

Lovingly lifting each name to Christ

He has all honor, power, and glory

He alone is worthy to be praised

Holy, Holy, Holy, is the Lord God Almighty

The Other Bread

1 Peter 4:17 For the time has come for judgment to begin at the house of God; and if it begins with us first, what will be the end of those who do not obey the gospel of God?

Galatians 5: 19-21 speaks on the different temptations of the flesh. sexual immorality, impurity, lustful pleasures, idolatry, sorcery, hostility, quarreling, jealousy, outbursts of anger, selfish ambition, rebellion, division, envy, drunkenness, wild parties, and other sins like these.

Galatians chapter 5 comes with a warning that says; let me tell you again, as I have before, that anyone living that sort of life will not inherit the Kingdom of God.

I've learned through reading Gods word that judgment should always begin with me. My desire should be: I should be warned by God first then, as He instructs me to warn others, isn't that what John the Baptist did?

What's Gnashing

I have all sort of what I call lessons God gives me to ponder upon and then write about. One day I woke up and within fifteen minutes I found myself in the middle of an argument. A few minutes later I turned on the radio and someone was quoting Psalms twenty-two about being gnashed at with teeth. Then about an hour later two dogs tried to bite me within a half an hour of each other. Now this all got my attention real quick I thought about dogs trying to bite someone. Two days later I had someone sitting next to me at bible study pointed to a scripture. I looked and was amazed. It was **Revelations 22:15 But outside are dogs and**

sorcerers and sexually immoral and murderers and idolaters, and whoever loves and practices a lie. I said, why did you show me that scripture? She said, because I thought it was funny. Well I sure didn't think it was funny at all. I really didn't know what to think. I only knew God was trying to tell me something. I knew this scripture it's about those denied access to the city of heaven. I thought how someone can think this is funny. I sought desperately to understand what God was trying to show me.

Then it all came together as I read **Psalms 37:12-13 The wicked plots against the just, and gnashes at him with his teeth. The Lord laughs at him, for He sees that his day is coming.** I thought, Gods laughing here, isn't He?

The Book of Jude Clarifies Gnashing

Please read the book of Jude. The book of Jude has only twenty five powerful verses which speak of two kinds of people those who have corruption within themselves and those who Jude calls the beloved.

Note: If it's possible the very elect of God may be deceived. There are those around us that have crept into the church that are ungodly. They may appear to be Godly, but they are harsh and not gentle and are corrupting the holiness and love of God. Jude goes as far to call them filthy dreamers in verse eight. I speak of this all to make one point where is our daily bread coming from. Holy or unholy words spoken into our lives verse eighteen states, there are mockers who twist themselves to appear to have the Spirit of God, but truly are sensual not having His Spirit. Verse twenty states, we the beloved must keep ourselves built up praying in the Holy Spirit of God and to always walk in the love of God and looking for His mercy. We mustn't allow ourselves to become offended and step out of love and gnash and rail against any. In verse nine even the archangel of God Michael didn't dare to rail accusations against the devil. If an angel of God knew better than to rail against God's own adversary instead said, the Lord rebuke you. We must not rail against one another.

Ecclesiastes speaks of times and seasons that produce a lack of usefulness with no importance. This sums things up for those damaging words which gnash and produce no life in the kingdom of God.

There was a time to cast stones under the old covenant and it had its purpose under the Law of Moses.

Now is the time of the new covenant between God and man which is the Law of Spirit in the life of Christ Jesus which speaks; it's time to gather stones. Our words must be gentle, loving and kind creating no harm to our fellow mans soul.
(Romans 8:12, Ecclesiastics 3:5)

Romans 13:8-10

owe no one anything except to love one another, for he who loves another has fulfilled the law. For the commandments, You shall not commit adultery, You shall not murder, You shall not steal, You shall not bear false witness, You shall not covet, and if there is any other commandment, are all summed up in this saying, namely, You shall love your neighbor as yourself. Love does no harm to a neighbor; therefore love is the fulfillment of the law.

Chapter 8
Forgive Us Our Trespasses

Whose Child Is This

I had gone to hear an old friend speak and a woman came up for prayer. She was over whelmed thinking about her unsaved son, so she asked those in the meeting to prayer for his salvation. The speaker was very persistent and repeatedly asked the question, do you have a daughter? The woman each time would reply, I don't have one, and she'd start pleading for her son's soul again. Finally the speaker gained her attention and asked, Are you sure you don't have a daughter? Finally she stated, my husband has a daughter. The speaker asked the girl's name and she became the focus of everyone's prayer. Later on that evening my spirit was concerned that this woman didn't acknowledge the girl as her own daughter. The Lord spoke in my spirit, <u>there are three ways we receive our children; the first by natural birth, the second by foster care or adoption, and the third by marriage.</u>

Before I go any further I feel should speak about my ignorance and lawlessness according to God's Word.

Matthew 24:12 And because lawlessness will abound, the love of many will grow cold.

Lawlessness: against the law, referring to the Law of Moses in this context of iniquity or sin

Lawlessness is an unusual word in today's society. I wanted to use it to illustrate a better picture of the words iniquity, disorder, and violation of God's law.

I have grown in the knowledge of God's Word, but only by studying and hearing it. I was very ignorant to His principles because I was not trained with much biblical wisdom. Any understanding that has come forth has come from reading, studying, and meditating on the Word of God as an adult.

Through my own ignorance of lawlessness by premarital sexual relations I like many today bore a child outside of marriage. Then I married and had a second child, I divorced and married again and had two more children which make a total of four children. The point of this information is whose children are they? This was an aggressive argument in my own household.

You're not my father!

This is my house and you're going to listen to me!

They're my children I'll do the disciplining!

Keep your hands off my kids!

This is the status quo in many homes today broken by lawlessness. Good News! We survived and they know that they all our children and an equal part of this family.

During the course of time many through offense and have allowed their love to wax cold and break the covenant of their marriage vow. They have fallen into the pattern of marriage then divorce and another marriage or never marrying at all.

There are those who have bore children before marriage through fornication and those who have been tempted to commit adultery that subsequently brings a child into their marriage. Ignorance and guilt plays the same game through pre-marital fornication and post-marital adultery they both are a result of temptation and lack of self control.

The children brought into these relationships have been made to feel they are partially owned by the new spouse or even unwanted. They are spoken of as step children or yours and not mine. I believe God was addressing this as he had my friend repeatedly ask the woman, are you sure you don't have a daughter? She finally responded with my husband has a daughter.

Trust Worthy

When we accept our spouse, our marriage becomes covenant, and what was once mine now becomes ours; there is no dividing point.

We must understand God's Kingdom is under His authority and governed by His holy commandments. When we accept Jesus we become co-heirs with Him in the Kingdom of Heaven. To be co-heirs means to fully own and believe together on the same inheritance. Co-heirs means the inheritance is ours entirely with no division. Co-heirs have no place or dividing point where they divvy up the inheritance. If it happens that you have any need of the inheritance it's at your disposal no questions asked, because everyone is trust worthy.

I had the opportunity to write this woman a letter. Boldly I put in simple words that she was to look after and mother her new daughter the same as she would the son she was weeping for. I explained how she through the marriage covenant became this child's mother.

In the family of God there is no division. It's kind of like the community pot all contribute, all partake, and no one misuses. We can't take apart families or fail to give and receive love. This indifference is cruel to the soul leaving wounds of rejection that only a covenant care can repair. It is never too late to add love to the pot. Remember, I'm sorry goes a long way. Some things can't be explained because some actions don't have excuses. The truth is we can't explain why some thing's ever occurred. We have to forgive and forget to carry on. So if no explanation can be produced we have to say truthfully I just don't know why. That's where Gods love and His merciful ways must be accepted. Prayer is the ultimate tool when all that can be done has been done. God will make a way for the rest.

I asked my son one day do you remember as you were growing up all the questions you had and the times that I was too busy talking to someone else and you never asked them? My son's reply was, yes. I said, I'm so sorry, with tears in my eyes.

Yes, we all get busy and distracted, but at what cost? There is so much going on moment by moment and what do we choose to give our attention to?

We need to get this order clear.

#1God

#2 our spouse

#3 our children

#4 others

Prayer: Oh! Father God, through your Holy Spirit, I pray you reveal all I need to see and do for the healing of my own children. In Jesus name I ask this gift of sight Amen.

Listening and Speaking

At times we do the very opposite that God the Father and His son Jesus did as they communicated with each other. As we get absorbed with what ever is at hand, our response becomes altered. If one could fully give attention to all that is thrown at us in a moment, our responses would be different. There are so many distractions that occur even in a moment of time that discernment from God is necessary to make a correct decision. It is not okay to ignore our God given responsibility to our children.

All Kinds of Reactions and Emotions Have Been Produced When a Child is Being Ignored and Left to Wander in Their Own Way

When I didn't feel I had attention or had been given the place to communicate as a child I seldom went back with my situation at hand. In other words I might have had a bad situation I just encountered and felt no one cares and kept silent. We have to discern when to listen to our children, because a child <u>learns</u> to feel their situations are not important to the adult.

Our relationships must first become complete in Godly principles. We aren't conformed into the image of God just by accepting Jesus into our heart. Only by daily reading the Bible and spending different moments throughout the day quietly in prayer we begin to hear His voice. Ones faith comes by hearing the Word of God and by listening to God who speaks with a still small voice within the heart. It is every act, every moment, every day, learning what God is communicating to us and being faithful to Him daily that conforms ones heart. **(Romans 10:17)**

Proverbs 29: 15 The rod and rebuke give wisdom, But a child left to himself brings shame to his mother.

As a child learns to make their own decisions, they may listen to a stranger or new found friend without knowing if it's right or wrong. Good daily communication is a must. The parent protecting the child needs to every day identify what has been presented to a child. We must focus on our greatest duty our children, or they may never get time to say, did you know this happened today?

As a parent myself I have looked back to see different things which troubled my own household. I can see the effects my children have endured by my parental ignorance.

I love my children with all my heart. I like most parents became preoccupied entertaining different people during the course of time trying to gain friendships. Diligence must lie in watching our own kingdom. Yes we do have a duty to our fellowman, but first we must serve our own household.

As a child I accepted the idea it was best not to bother adults when they were dealing with something much more important than what I had to say. That accepted concept was acquired by a little girl who had no idea how important her parents really thought she was. My parents never knew I felt that way. Nevertheless I did. I know my parents would have done everything they possibly could to communicate better, if they realized I didn't know how to.

God Desires to Adopt us as His Children

Ephesians1:5-6 Having predestined us to adoption as sons by Jesus Christ to Himself, according to the good pleasure of His will, to the praise of the glory of His grace, by which He made us accepted in the Beloved.

We must realize God's motivation for adoption. He knew in advance that there would be those who would ask Him to change their hearts to be pleasing and acceptable to him. What more could a Father want than a child who would choose His ways?

The Kings Son

The boy said father and the crowd hushed giving reverence to the voice of the son

As they all knew when a child of the king speaks all other business is put aside

The father didn't want to fail in any important daily lesson that may be arising from the inner most being of his son

Yes, my child what can I do as he turns to communicate with the young man

Each time he has a new question everything else falls to the side of the father's attention

Diligence must prevail to prepare for the son's future reign as King

Teaching obedience and mastering this skill is his only purpose

I do what I see my father doing was his reply

Chapter 9

Surely Goodness

Lamentations 3:22-26 Through the LORD's mercies we are not consumed, because His compassions fail not. They are new every morning; great is your faithfulness. The LORD is my portion, says my soul, Therefore I hope in Him! The LORD is good (towb) to those who wait for Him, to the soul who seeks Him.

The Knowledge of His goodness Reflects the Presence of His Light

What is goodness and how does God's goodness apply to our lives? His goodness applied to one's life proves to be beneficial in creating healing and abundant life. So I've compiled a number of the original meanings to the word goodness to confirm Gods goodness toward His creation of man.

Goodness :(towb) to be good, pleasing, joyful, beneficial, pleasant, favorable, happy, right

Exodus 18:9 Then Jethro rejoiced for all the good (towb) which the LORD had done for Israel, whom He had delivered out of the hand of the Egyptians.

This scripture is taken from an event in the biblical history of Israel. Now Israel was formed through God's holy covenant with Abraham and his seed. Abraham was the father of Isaac. Isaac was the father of Jacob. God changed Jacob's name to Israel. These are the original people who formed the nation of Israel. Through the course of time the people Israel became slaves under the Egyptian Pharaoh. Because of God's covenant with Abraham He showed mercy and answered their cries of distress. God brought the people of Israel out of Egypt through a man called Moses. Gods opened a safe passage for the children of Israel to leave Egypt by parting the Red Sea. The Egyptian people tried to follow Israel through the Red Sea but the waters drew back overtook and destroyed them. When Jethro, Moses' father in-law, heard what God had done for Israel he came to visit Moses. At the sight of all the delivered people of Israel Jethro had to rejoice at the goodness of God.

Our Glimpse of Goodness

Goodness: (tuwb) good, pleasant, agreeable, rich, valuable in estimation, appropriate, becoming, better by comparative, glad, happy, prosperous, benign, good things, collective, wealth, fairer, favor, precious

Exodus 33:19 Then He said, I will make all my goodness (tuwb) pass before you, and I will proclaim the name of the LORD before you. I will be gracious to whom I will be gracious, and I will have compassion on whom I will have compassion.

Psalms 27:13 I would have lost heart, unless I had believed that I would see the goodness (tuwb) of the LORD In the land of the living.

The psalmist or King David wrote, **I would have lost heart**. He knew we needed to see Gods goodness now in this life. To some it may seem as if God is picking and choosing who He shows His goodness to. It is to the contrary seeing He was good to all men in offering escape from His wrath when He sent His son Jesus. It is according to our faith to believe who He is. But not all will choose to believe God to receive the full benefits of his goodness. He has chosen to be good to all men, the choice becomes ours by entering into covenant with him or not. You see if we don't choose to receive Christ as our Savior and obey the Word of God we haven't formed a covenant relationship with Him and His goodness is being rejected by us.

His Goodness Through Forgiveness

Goodness: (chrestos) fit for use, virtuous, manageable, pleasant, not harsh or bitter, benevolent

Goodness:(chrestotes) moral goodness, integrity, kindness

Romans 2:4 Or do you despise the riches of His goodness (chrestotes), forbearance, and longsuffering, not knowing that the goodness (chrestos) of God leads you to repentance?

Matthew 11:30 For My yoke [is] easy (chrestos), and My burden is light.

When we rebel against God and despise His wise counsel which is the Word of God we go into captivity or a yoke which binds us to that rebellion. This rebellion follows after things that are not like God. It could be anything that takes our attention away from God and what is good (chrestotes) and holy. In following the thing un-like God we begin to walk the way of the rebellious. Those who make this choice are opposing and defying Gods authority in order to accept a social status to stay part of the world's crowd.

Romans 13:8-10 Let every soul be subject to the governing authorities. For there is no authority except from God, and the authorities that exist are appointed by God. Therefore whoever resists the authority resists the ordinance of God, and those who resist will bring judgment on themselves. For

rulers are not a terror to good works, but to evil. Do you want to be unafraid of the authority? Do what is good, and you will have praise from the same.

So how do we escape Gods judgment? We don't except through repentance. There's no place to hide from what He has established in His word. We have a God so good (chrestos) that He leads us to repentance. Submitting to His leading is the only way to escape His judgment. God Himself set the law on how we are to act differently than the other nations. We should not embrace the sins of the nations, but pursue the will of God. What we His people must understand is that all the nations have gathered together by migration and the sins of all the nations have been carried everywhere. Without knowing His word we have just accepted it all as normal not knowing what God through His Word has to say.

Jesus also known as the Word of God (**John 1:14**) came to give sight to the spiritually blind, open the prison doors of those bound to sin and set at liberty those who are bruised by this world, on order to set those captive to sin, free. (**Luke 4:18**)

Jesus paid the price for all sin. God is just waiting for us to see that sin is not good. His wish is that no one should perish but all come to repentance and salvation through Jesus Christ our Lord.

Goodness: (agathopoieo) do good, well doing, do well

God is Good to the Unthankful and Evil

Luke 6:35 But love your enemies, do good (agathopoieo), and lend, hoping for nothing in return; and your reward will be great, and you will be sons of the Most High. For He is kind (chrestos) to the unthankful and evil.

God is good to all His creation. Jesus died and paid for everyone's sin. It's not Gods fault that people go their own way and reject His arrangement for salvation. Kindness is a fruit of the Spirit which considers others and is not cruel. God is not cruel or mean He always loves. We must be kind to our enemies, because this will show the love of God in us. We as His people will stand out as having a goodness that they don't understand. Be kind (chrestos) to your enemies, not devouring them with harshness, but with the attitude of Christ. Love your enemies bless those who curse you. **(Matthew 5:44)**

Goodness :(agathosyne) upright in heart and life, goodness, kindness

Goodness: (eudokia) will, choice, delight, satisfaction, desire

It is Good to Walk in the Holy Spirit

Romans 8:1-2 There is therefore now no condemnation to those who are in Christ Jesus, who do not walk according to the flesh, but according to the Spirit. For the law of the Spirit of life in Christ Jesus has made me free from the law of sin and death.

The Law of sin and death is a set of rules that God specifically gave the children of Israel through the voice of Moses. Through the sacrifice of Jesus a new law was established which sets one free from the law of sin and death. Through Gods grace He sent us Jesus who took the penalty of the law upon Himself. In receiving Jesus Christ as Lord and Savior we can now walk in His Spirit of love, which consist of joy, peace, longsuffering, kindness, goodness, faithfulness, gentleness (agathosyne), and self-control. **(Galatians 5:22)**

Galatians 6:2 Bear one another's burdens, and so fulfill the law of Christ.

Through the goodness of God we have become His children. It gives pleasure to God to see us fulfill the work of faith with power truly being our brother's keeper in love.

Ephesians 2:5-6 But God, who is rich in mercy, because of His great love with which He loved us, even when we were dead in trespasses, made us alive together with Christ (by grace you have been saved), that in the ages to come He might show the exceeding riches of His grace in His kindness (chrestotes) **toward us in Christ Jesus.**

Only by Gods goodness has the life of Jesus come to us. This goodness of God's is what gives anything its estimated value. It is what makes things pleasant, favorable, joyful, and most precious. His goodness develops one into an agreeable and manageable person someone who's benign and not cancerous. We should be children pleasing in his sight, full of the wealth of His nature, cultivating a good moral character, being upright in heart and life, pleasant and not harsh, full of virtue, fit for His use. This is what pleases Him.

Goodness is Patient and Suffers Long Teach us to be Agreeable

I sat with a lady during lunch one day. She was tearing apart this piece of chicken bit by bit to feed her daughter. With every piece of chicken she'd ask, what do you want, more chicken? Then she turned and looked at me and said, I'm trying to teach her patience. Sounds good and looks good yes, but this maybe questionable by some as to whether or not the child was actually learning patience. I believe she was learning to be manageable.

To have to watch, wait, and listen, before receiving anything takes endurance. That child was agreeable and manageable, but why? The relationship she was forming with her mother.

Acquiring Gentle Goodness

Psalms 119:66 Teach me good (tuwb) judgment and knowledge, for I believe Your commandments.

James 1:19-20 So then, my beloved brethren, let every man be swift to hear, slow to speak, slow to wrath; for the wrath of man does not produce the righteousness of God.

The fruit of Gods Holy Spirit is good and it produces the righteousness of God. **(Psalms 34:8)** Just as in mans physical body fruit cleanses impurities and causes health and strength. The fruit of Gods Spirit cleanses and strengthens mans soul and spirit. I have struggled with being patient and responding with gentleness in frustrating situations. This fruit of the Spirit had not been cultivated in me as a child so as an adult sporadic fruit was produced through me. Being gentle one minute and harsh the next minute causes despair in ones spirit. It is the stability of loving others enough to guard their hearts at all cost that pure fruit comes forth. Without a fixed productive gentleness anger can come forth in abundance.

Ephesians 5:9-11 For the fruit of the Spirit is in all goodness (agathosyne) and righteousness and truth. Finding out what is acceptable to the Lord. And have no fellowship with the unfruitful works of darkness, but rather expose them.

To look back and see the damage anger had produced has its effects on the soul. One must weigh the production of things by examination of cause and effect. If we could see the outcome of an action beforehand one would be more cautious not to act harshly.

Now that I see how progression has flowed through the generations of my life: from my parents, to myself, then to my children and grandchildren. I look at the words, <u>train up a child in the way they should go.</u> We must truly see what we have been trained to be. To be gentle or not be gentle that is my question? So I have determined at all cost, I must lay down my life and become gentle in order to exhibit the righteousness of God for those around me. I have realized if I think I'm going to be gentle in all situations and something should happen to cause me to fail, I would condemn myself. This struggle has exposed a truth I can never assume to remain gentle in my own power, but only by the grace of God and His Holy Spirit can I have any self control.

<u>Try It! You'll Like It.!</u>

When the family as a whole is retrained to act mercifully toward each other in Gods gentleness great results are produced. Remember without love we are just a loud annoying noise.
(1Corinthians Chapter 13)

Luke 10:25-28 He said to him, what is written in the law? What is your reading of it? So he answered and said, you shall love the LORD your God with all your heart, with all your soul, with all your strength, and with all your mind, and your neighbor as yourself. And He said to him, you have answered rightly; do this and you will live.

Romans 15: 14 Now I myself am confident concerning you, my brethren, that you also are full of goodness (agathosyne) filled with all knowledge, able also to admonish one another."

2 Thessalonians 1:11 Therefore we also pray always for you that our God would count you worthy of this calling, and fulfill all the good pleasure (eudokia) of His goodness (agathosyne), and the work of faith with power.

Prayer: Dear Father give to us your Wisdom From Above that is Pure, Peaceable, Gentle, Willing to Yield, Full of Mercy and Good Fruits, Without Partiality and Without Hypocrisy. Now the Fruit of Righteousness is Sown in Peace by those who Make Peace. Amen. (James 3:17-18)

Chapter 10

Defining Honor

Where Does Honor Start

Honor: hold in high esteem

Rebellion: attempt to overthrow government, defiance of authority

God will not always strive with man. He has made the way to walk in peace and honor toward Him the choice is ours. As one gains Godly knowledge we should separate ourselves from the things God says are abominable. God Himself has reveal the honorable way to the man He has created. We either accept it or reject it. The choice is ours. Through the Holy Spirit one can gain the wisdom, knowledge, and understanding to fear God and not strive against Him with a hard heart.

Job 9:2-4 Truly I know it is so, But how can a man be righteous before God? If one wished to contend with Him, He could not answer Him one time out of a thousand. God is wise in heart and mighty in strength. Who has hardened himself against Him and prospered?

1. We are dealing with honor in this chapter. David was un-faithful to his fellow man.

2. King David in the book Samuel through lust and temptation committed several ungodly acts.

3. By being the King of Israel he was suppose to be leading the people in the righteousness of God.

4. David was a man after God's heart who desired to do things Gods way.

5. David lived under the Law of Moses which meant that if you sinned the result was death.

6. We today aren't under the law but Gods grace where He is continually speaking to repent and stop sinning like David did.

The Cleansing of David's Soul

(2 Samuel chapter 11 & 12) This story begins…God sent Nathan the prophet to speak to David about the affair he had with Bathsheba and how he tried to cover his sin of getting another man's wife pregnant. David sent for Uriah her husband who was away at war. David met with Uriah and after his meeting he told him go home and enjoy your wife, Uriah who was faithful to the king and his army wouldn't go. So David resorted to send a letter with Uriah to have his enemies kill him in battle.

2 Samuel 11:14 And he wrote in the letter, saying, Set Uriah in the forefront of the hottest battle, and retreat from him, that he may be struck down and die.

2 Samuel 12:13-14 So David said to Nathan, I have sinned against the LORD. And Nathan said to David, the LORD also has put away your sin; you shall not die. However, because by this deed you have given great occasion to the enemies of the LORD to blaspheme, the child also who is born to you shall surely die.

David Hardened not His Heart

The following point… David fasted and prayed trying to change Gods decision concerning the child's death. Yes, David contended with God trying to change His mind. When David saw the completion of his sin that ultimitly brought forth the death of Uriah and Bathsheba's child. He washed himself and accepted Gods righteous judgment and didn't harden himself against God. Because David had a heart full of repentance the Lord put away his sin. **(2Samuel chapter 7)**

Luke 1:32-33 He will be great, and will be called the Son of the Highest; and the Lord God will give Him the throne of His father David. And He will reign over the house of Jacob forever, and of His kingdom there will be no end.

Hebrews 12: 5-11 demonstrates that we have earthly fathers who chastise us after their own pleasure. We also have a Heavenly Father who corrects after His own pleasure as sons and daughters not as illegitimate children. We are partakers of His holiness producing the fruit of His righteousness. We can't argue with a God who is mighty in heart and strength. He is not an unjust ogre. Moreover He is merciful. We don't get what we deserve and cannot argue with His righteousness David didn't.

Job Feared God and Hated Evil

Job 42:1-7 Then Job answered the LORD and said: I know that You can do everything, And that no purpose of Yours can be withheld from You. You asked Who is this who hides counsel without knowledge? Therefore I have uttered what I did not understand, Things too wonderful for me, which I did not know. Listen, please, and let me speak; You said, I will question you, and you shall answer Me. I have heard of You by the hearing of the ear, But now my eye sees You. Therefore I abhor myself, and repent in dust and ashes. And so it was, after the LORD had spoken these words to Job that the LORD said to Eliphaz the Terminate My wrath is aroused against you

and your two friends, for you have not spoken of Me what is right, as My servant Job has.

Job had to learn that all that we think, know, and understand of Gods ways; are too wonderful for us to fully comprehend. Through study of the Word of God we should also understand; until we see God face to face no one can fully comprehend the purpose behind His plans. We must simply have faith in God. Sure we get clips of vision, but even at that just the shadow of the purpose is revealed in this life time. Yes, we can accomplish many things for God, but all power comes by His Hand. Job had no control over the wind that came and took his children. He had no power to heal himself or convince his comforters he had a well-regarded honor for God. God is the only one who can reveal such things. In the end God revealed Job's heart for Him publicly and doubly restored all that he had. In Jobs conclusion of his own personal matters he should always maintain a respectful honor to God.

God and His Honor to His own Word

Hebrews 11:3/a By faith we understand that the worlds were framed by the word of God, so that the things which are seen were not made of things which are visible.

Establish: set up, place something permanently, and confirm truth

Through faith we understand that the worlds were framed by the word of God, The word worlds comes from a Greek meaning of ages. We can by faith know that the ages were adjusted by a word from God. All foundations were formed by God, He established all things.

God spoke and it was complete from beginning to end. This is what makes Him Alpha and Omega. With His Word He set all the ages in order, all measures and weights, times and distance, laws and orders. God is honorable to that Word, because He does not change and He is performing what He said. We can trust His Word which has been established as truth.

Job 38:4-6 Where were you when I laid the foundations of the earth? Tell Me, if you have understanding. Who determined its measurements? Surely you know! Or who stretched the line upon it? To what were its foundations fastened? Or who laid its cornerstone.

Who can answer that nobody, but God and God alone? This is what Job finally understood through the knowledge and wisdom he gained from God.

The Order of Jesus

Isaiah 11:2 The Spirit of the LORD shall rest upon Him, The Spirit of wisdom and understanding, The Spirit of counsel and might, The Spirit of knowledge and of the fear of the LORD.

Hebrew 1:2-3 GOD, who at various times and in various ways spoke in time past to the fathers by the prophets, has in these last days spoken to us by His Son, whom He has appointed heir of all things, through whom also He made the worlds; who being the brightness of His glory and the express image of His person, and upholding all things by the word of His power, when He had by Himself purged our sins, sat down at the right hand of the Majesty on high,

Uphold: to maintain, defend, to provide moral support, inspire somebody with confidence, especially laws or principles

God fulfilled His honor to us through the sacrifice of His own Son. Jesus honored His Father's word, without a fight. By honor Jesus was obedient to go to the garden and say, Father not my will but yours be done. By honor Jesus allowed His soul to go on trial for all mankind's redemption. By honor Jesus allowed Himself to be handled by angry men to suffer brutal abuse unto the point of death. Jesus honored His Father because; He was confident His Father would raise Him back alive to His side in heaven. By faith, honor, and full obedience Jesus said it was finished and all debt and redemption for mankind was fulfilled through His honoring His Father's Word. Jesus was saying, Daddy, the job is done your way.

All God expects of us is to be individually lead by His Word and Spirit for His purpose.

I as a parent expect obedience. There is nothing more satisfying in my own relationships with my children then to speak and observe my child has listened to my words. No argument, no explanation needed, just faithfully in a timely manner carrying out my instruction without adding their ideas to my request.

Jesus the Example of Gods Honor

2 Samuel 22:31 As for God, His way is perfect; The word of the LORD is proven; He is a shield to all who trust in Him.

The first chapter of John explains how Jesus is the Word. Samuel in the above scripture declares that Gods ways are perfect and His Word is proven. Well, if Jesus is the Word then God proved His way was perfect to offer Jesus as sins remedy.

John1:33-34 And John bore witness, saying, "I saw the Spirit

descending from heaven like a dove, and He remained upon Him I did not know Him, but He who sent me to baptize with water said to me, upon whom you see the Spirit descending, and remaining on Him, this is He who baptizes with the Holy Spirit.

The prophets of old kept pointing to Jesus the Messiah. Now King David's beloved coming King, was standing face to face with John to be baptized. Suddenly the Holy Spirit manifested its self and descended on Jesus. God the Father manifested Himself by opening the heavens and speaking this is my beloved son, in whom I am well pleased. The Father, son, and Holy Spirit all came together in front of one man, John, to publicly show in agreement that this is the one you can trust in. **(Mathew 3:16-17)**

Looking back to **(Hebrews 1:2-3)** I can see Jesus was who the Father appointed: the heir and creator of all things, shining with The Fathers glory, expressing the Father's image, and upholding all things by His Fathers Word of power. Alone He purged us from our sins and now rests in majesty on high.

Jesus defended His Fathers creation, glory, image, and the power of His Word by facing all adversity. He had to divide and discern every thought and intention to be the eternal defender.

Hebrews 4:12 The Word of God is quick and powerful, and sharper than any two-edged sword, piercing even to the dividing asunder of soul and spirit, and of the joints and marrow, and is a discerner of the thoughts and intents of the heart. (King James Version)

Man and His Honor

1 Peter 2:17 Honor all people. Love the brotherhood. Fear God. Honor the King.

We need to exercise Godly patience with one another. Remember in the introduction to this book Jesus was filled with compassion for the multitude. He views us as sheep needing a Shepherd.

We observe those around us who were never taught about Jesus and His ways. Their outward appearance may shock us or their actions may offend us. But we need to ask ourselves who is the child inside that grew up with a broken down soul that still needs to be reached by Jesus. Those taught by the world void of the life and Spirit of Jesus these are our commission from God. We are to honor all people, love the brotherhood, fear God, and honor the king.

1. Honor all people means we can't pick and choose who we show honor to. God said, honor all people. We as followers of Christ can't ignore this. We can do this: by honoring those who have gone astray through sin as we care enough about their eternal souls to start praying for all men, Buddhist, Hindu, Muslim, tattooed, pierced, drunkard, and even murderers. Why did God choose to be so gracious to us? Why have we been blessed to already recognize Jesus as Savior? Can we think we are special? Our time to receive Jesus was our time. If they will come to Him, that will be their time. It's not our place to look at or listen to others' judgments of the people of this world. If we do we'll never care. We know the truth about Jesus, but they still are ignorant. We must remember when we were ignorant and how gracious He was to us. Its pride to think God honors one man more than any one else. Jesus paid for every one's souls and that means even those we believe could be the worst person. As believers in Christ Jesus we should be trusted to honor those he loves. In Luke chapter thirteen Jesus spoke about two separate events that had occurred. The first was about the Galileans which had been slain by Pilate while offering sacrifices and the eighteen who died when the tower of Siloam fell. Jesus wanted to know if they supposed these were the worst sinners in the area. He said, Not at all! Unless you repent of your sins and turn to God you also will all perish. In other words we better be concerned with our own sins and repent.

2. Love the brotherhood our wonderful family of believers who recognize Jesus Christ as Lord and Savior. The word says they will know we are Christians by are love for each other.

3. Fear God, He has established His Word and He doesn't change. What He said is law. He is merciful and gracious, but He is not to be reckoned with.

4. Honor the King: What ever country you're from be faithful to pray for your government leader, your country's personal reigning king.

1 John 2:5 But whoever keeps His word, truly the love of God is perfected in him. By this we know that we are in Him.

When mans disobedience to God occurred, peace between God and man dissolved. God could not allow man to live forever in his new sinful state; so God removed mans access to the tree of life. Why, Because He didn't want us to have to deal with sin forever. **(Genesis 2:17) (Genesis 3:22-24)**

The same opposition that worked on man to ignore God in the beginning is still working against mankind today. We have become so used to others thoughts and ways directing our paths that many don't even consider God's voice. It should be His voice that has the first and last word in our lives. Yes, there are those chosen by God to speak His wisdom into our lives. But man should understand that we all individually need to seek God daily.

Jesus' honor to God demonstrated to us how to obey God's voice. When Jesus needed direction He went straight to the Father and came back with actions of obedience. This is why He is known as the way, the truth, and the life. He said, I can do nothing by myself except what I see the Father do. His ways are true and they will lead us back to Gods life. **(John 5:19)**

After the resurrection of Jesus the twelve apostles became our example, by showing their individual obedience to the Father in step after Jesus. The church was built on this foundation for every other follower of Christ to take the gospel to the world.
(Ephesians 2:20, Revelations 21:14)

Our Struggles With Gods Word

Ephesians 6:12 For we do not wrestle against flesh and blood, but against principalities, against powers, against the rulers of the darkness of this age, against spiritual hosts of wickedness in the heavenly places.

The battle one struggles against is not the ordinary daily people who oppose us. The Word of Gods says it's against these different levels of opposing demons of the devil. The whole focus of the opposition is; if at all possible undermined the things of God through deception.

Undermine: to discredit, to diminish or weaken something gradually by malicious action

Without the light of Gods Word man has been taught many ungodly principles. Learning His principles for handling our lives will change every belief and attitude one has held in the past by His truth.

We must remember we are new creations in Christ the old life is past and a new life has begun. **(2 Corinthians 5:17)**

Rebellion to Gods Always Pierces our own Life

The comprehension of Godly principles has been difficult for those that have been taught, if they haven't earned my respect I'm not going to give it to them. This is a false principle against the Word of God.

We cannot hold onto ungodly attitudes or reject His Word without being in rebellion to Him.

Authority has Been Abused by Mankind

No one should have ever override God's authority to overpower another person. Some people in authority believe they just have the right to use cruelty to get someone to conform to them. It's the different levels of opposing demons against one soul that are trying to teach us to rebel and not conform to God. If they can present the element to doubt toward the Word of God then the battle that wars within the soul is on. Just like Eve and the serpent in the garden, the serpent said, did God really say that? The serpent spoke the element of doubt by challenging the spoken word which caused Eve to doubt what God really said. If we don't read the Word of

God for our selves what do we really know? No wonder there is so much doubt and unbelief in the hearts of men, because they don't know for sure what God has said within their own heart.

John 10:10 The thief does not come except to steal, and to kill, and to destroy. I have come that they may have life, and that they may have it more abundantly.

Jesus knew the Word of God. He never allowed anything to build itself on the already established foundation of that Word. When the devil came to tempt Jesus He had the truth already formed within His heart. With a steadfast heart for that Word doubt and unbelief could not be manifested even though it tried.

We must learn to listen to Gods voice individually and follow it without letting any other words interfere with His direction.

People just interject their opinion so fast when ones trials come; if not living and knowing the Word of God those words will try to dominate our thought process. Man has been taught to run to another man's voice, before running to God. Then when left to our own plans without seeking Him, trouble occurs. Some will get angry and blame God for the mess while, God had no participation in the situation.

Honoring God's Word Dominates the Factor they Don't Deserve Respect.

We must learn to consult God and to follow His instruction, one must diligently inquire what does the Word of God say? Those led by the Spirit are the children of God.

Most of our rebellion towards God forms as a child. Spite and rebellion deeply roots itself within our hearts at a very young age. People who are looking for revenge will always function out of spite and rebellion. I guess you could call it kicking against the pricks. Then as we grow older we exhibit rebellion to most authority the first time we don't agree with their instructions.

When a person who is in authority (usually a parent, grandparent, teacher, or boss ...) brings disgrace to the one they are leading, respect for that person may become lost.

When any one chooses to remember an offense and won't turn it loose, their honor is misplaced. If a loss of respect for authority should occur. Once confidence in that person is lost; rebellion to their authority usually takes over. So most things they would direct one to do might be disobeyed, because the peace and honor towards that person has been interrupted. Usually God gets the blame for connecting us with that leader in the first place. So when rebellion towards that person occurs they unconsciously connect it to God and start rebelling against His word.

Hebrews 13:17 Obey those who rule over you, and be submissive, for they watch out for your souls, as those who must give account. Let them do so with joy and not with grief, for that would be unprofitable for you.

The element that most people may be unaware of is that those who rule us **are supposed to be watching out for our souls.** King David watched out for his kingdom. The prophets were watching out for the rulers so they wouldn't lead people astray from what God expected of them. Pastors are watching out for their congregations, parents their children and teachers their students. It is much easier for us to look at like this; **Honor God** by honoring those He has chosen on earth who are suppose to watching over us. **God will deal with them**.

As one grows through reading the word of God and recognizes their rebellion towards Gods authority repentance should occur within the heart.

The New Focal Point

God word instructs us to obey those in authority over us as obeying Him.

When we disobey those God has commanded us to honor we disobey God.

All have experienced some minor or major offense affecting the order of authority. To lose respect for people will always happen, but God's order of honor must at all times remain unbroken.

When this revelation of disobedience comes to light we must repent and honor God by submitting to those He said to obey.

Through our repentance and obedience to Gods word we will see His peace return to our relationships.

Gods' kingdom is righteousness, peace, and joy.

We must follow after His righteousness or His right way to enjoy that peace and joy. **(Galatians 5:22)**

God's Order of Honoring Him
Colossians 3:17-25

Submit: fall into rank

Fitting: suitable or appropriate for the circumstances

Obey: to do as told, conform

Pleasing: satisfying

Love: show kindness

Bitter: resentful, hostile, acid comments, sarcastic

Provoke: to make someone feel angry, to be intentional

Discourage: to make somebody feel less motivated, unconfident, to dishearten

Eye service: agreeing with one's eyes not heart, therefore there's a careless service performance

Inheritance: legal inheritance, status, by being born into a particular family

Colossians 3:17-25 And whatever you do in word or deed, do all in the name of the Lord Jesus, giving thanks to God the Father through Him. Wives, <u>submit</u> to your own husbands, as is <u>fitting</u> in the Lord. Husbands <u>love</u> your wives and do not be <u>bitter</u> toward them. Children, <u>obey</u> your parents in all things, for this is well <u>pleasing</u> to the Lord. Fathers, do not <u>provoke</u> your children, lest they become <u>discouraged</u>. Bondservants, obey in all things your masters according to the flesh, not with

eye service, as men-pleasers, but in sincerity of heart, fearing God. And whatever you do, do it heartily, as to the Lord and not to men, knowing that from the Lord you will receive the reward of the inheritance; for you serve the Lord Christ. But he who does wrong will be repaid for what he has done, and there is no partiality.

Question: Would you listen to the next door neighbor like you would your own father or mother? Hey! Jami come take out my trash. No you're not part of that family. What happens if your parent asks you to do it? See the difference.

When anyone receives Jesus they are born into Gods family and therefore they receive an inheritance from God. Part of our inheritance is His word full of instruction He rewards us for honoring His Fatherly words. Just as in the natural family when we obey those we serve we get rewards of love and praise from each other. In refusal of an asked service we receive correction. God set this order of honor within our relationships and if broken, natural and spiritual consequences will always come.

Envy and Strife or Good Will

Philippians 1:15 Some indeed preach Christ even of envy and strife; and some also from good will.

The Apostle Paul was warning the church that misusing the Word of God will have its consequences.

Envy: to trouble the good or to work evil
Strife: causing contention
Good Will: of a kind intent

Using the Word of God with Honor

I know that I myself have misused the Word of God.

The Word of God is for teaching us how to live and love.

It's for correction once we see the truth it will change our ways.

It's for edification to build us up to do good.

Those around us can see straight through us when we speak out of envy and strife; this is the hypocrisy the world views.

When serving those around us God discerns the use of Christ we intend when we speak to others.

Hebrews 4:12 For the word of God is living and powerful, and sharper than any two-edged sword, piercing even to the division of soul and spirit, and of joints and marrow, and is a discerner of the thoughts and intents of the heart.

God Commands us to Speak with Love and not Provoke Others to Wrath

The misuse of Christ message disheartens those we love by not walking in God's love but, contention.

What kind of example of Christ have we portrayed?

In spite of hidden sin multitudes still have been saved and filled with the Holy Spirit.

The preachers who have hidden sin trying to exercise authority in reoccurring rebellion have deceived many into viewing them as truly righteous. Preaching Christ should produce Godly results but, if we are full of envy and strife when speaking, bitterness may be produced in the hearer.

We have to speak with a Godly intent to produce Gods love; therefore receiving a Godly response and not a rebellious reaction.

We should never feel we have an edge because our position in authority.

Jesus washed the disciples' feet and stated the servant is not greater than his lord. If, Christ could bow down his position to wash and serve we must also bow and serve with the heart of Christ. **(John 13:16)**

We should never feel we are above or beneath any family member; we need to bow when the Spirit of God bids us to do so. Sometimes we are called to serve parents, brothers, sisters, children, friends, or our church family members. Sometimes those around us need to see us move from whatever position we have been placed in to be humble and lowly for their souls to be restored.

There are those of us who have loved ones or others who are suppose to give us honor and it's just not happening.

Sure we all want to be adored and honored by those we watch over. Let's face it; we haven't always appeared adorable in our dealings with those we are in authority over.

If we want the heart of those we are in charge of we must act out of love.

We must give our heart in love like God and love will do its work.

I know when I act in wrath and not love all I have received is a bunch of head butting. Love has a voice worth listening to, it turns away wrath and gains us respect.

There are those who won't honor God ways and therefore a positive response is harder to obtain.

Love patiently washes that hardness away.

No matter what's going on we must always give, God's commands respect and obedience.

Honor is the Gold Refined and Fit For the Master's Use

If we truly begin to honor others as ourselves our relationship with God is back on track, Hallelujah!

The Church and its Honor

God's Word is established in and through the church. On receiving the in filling of the Spirit of God through acceptance of Jesus Christ, His Word begins to establish itself in us. We must honor God and allow His Word to do its work in us and then proceed out of us in order for Him to properly build His Church.

Ephesians 3:19 and to make all see what *is* the fellowship of the mystery, which from the beginning of the ages has been hidden in God who created all things through Jesus Christ;

Jesus' last spoken words upon the cross 'it is finished' come to life as they meet their appointed destination in each soul through out time. God sent His Word to accomplish what it was sent out to do, to judge between sin and righteousness. So where ever sin has taken hold throughout time Christ's salvation will be offered.

Ephesians 2:7 that in the ages to come He might show the exceeding riches of His grace in *His* kindness toward us in Christ Jesus.

The words it is finished God has been dispensed through the ages to accomplish all redemptions undertaking. **(Isaiah 55:11)**

Jesus shed His blood for all our lost souls. His word is moving through time reaching and healing all who will receive that word. God is no respecter of persons therefore we can't pick and choose who will be established as part of Gods church. For this purpose only has God established His church: to gather His people together in agreement through Christ.

Behold the Lamb of God Who Takes Away the Sins of the World

1 Corinthians 11:28-32 But let a man examine himself, and so let him eat of the bread and drink of the cup. For he who eats and drinks in an unworthy manner eats and drinks judgment to himself, not discerning the Lord's body. For this reason many are weak and sick among you, and many sleep. For if we would judge ourselves, we would not be judged. But when we are judged, we are chastened by the Lord, that we may not be condemned with the world."

I remember the first time I received communion. I wanted Jesus to be the Lord and Savior of every area of my life. I repented of my sins as fast as I could, to receive His forgiving atonement.

The second time I received communion, my mouth was filled with so much praise I received the baptism in the Holy Spirit. **(Acts 2:4)**

Then one day I heard the words in a sermon let a man examine himself with the warning he who eats unworthy. From that point somehow I felt condemned and unworthy every time I took communion. **(1 Corinthians 11:28-32)**

What went wrong?

I started examining my current struggles facing me at the time of receiving communion and condemnation crept in.

I thought I had to be totally sinless not to get sick to receive communion.

Wrong! The enemy was trying to bring weakness, sickness and the world's condemnation to my soul and keep me from receiving communion.

For years I privately thought I was a failure to Christ. It seemed every time I'd receive communion some symptom of weakness or sickness would flood my mind; I'd take it hook, line, and sinker as it was trying to separate me from the love of Jesus.

God finally got through to me; this world is already condemned or sick, weak, and dying without Jesus. He sent Jesus to save me from these things. I needed to see Jesus as the ultimate sacrifice broken by sin, He came for the sick, weak, and dying; to set us free and make us strong through His broken body.

John 3:17 For God did not send His Son into the world to condemn the world, but that the world through Him might be saved.

When Jesus died He bore our sins, He died as every individual type of sinner there is in the world throughout all ages. So, if He was replacing us as the sinner when He died, He took upon Himself our sins name; for example liar, thief, murder, and so on down the entire list. Jesus was broken for every sin known to man.

When I pictured Jesus had been broken for our restoration to God, I was aware that my sin was no different than all the sin of the world. I realized communion was remembering Jesus took all of the worlds sins and I am forgiven.

1 John 2:1-2 My little children, these things write I unto you, that ye sin not. And if any man sin, we have an advocate with the Father, Jesus Christ the righteous: And He Himself is the propitiation for our sins and not for ours only but also for the whole world.

No Greater Honor

Now as I sit to take communion, I remember what it cost for me to have fellowship with Jesus. He paid with His body and blood so we can spend an eternity with Him in heaven. His broken body brought the fullness of God back into our lives here on earth. Being a part of His body I must lay aside all human pride and accept whosoever also accepts Jesus. Just to realized that we all are equally loved and Jesus doesn't offer more of Himself to anyone.

Some think they are greater and others think they are less we just need to know that He loves us the same. That we don't have to compete for His love just obey His request to love God and one another as we love ourselves and feed His sheep.
(Luke 10:27-28, John 21:16-17)

Luke 22:19 And He took bread, gave thanks and broke it, and gave it to them, saying, This is My body which is given for you; do this in remembrance of Me.

John 15:13 Greater love has no one than this, than to lay down one's life for his friends.

John 13:5-8 After that, He poured water into a basin and began to wash the disciples feet, and to wipe them with the towel with which He was girded. Then He came to Simon Peter. And Peter said to Him, Lord, are You washing my feet? Jesus answered and said to him, What I am doing you do not understand now, but you will know after this. Peter said to Him, You shall never wash my feet! Jesus answered him, If I do not wash you, you have no part with Me.

Jesus washed the disciples' feet and stated, to Peter if I do not wash you, you have no part in me. We all have walked through many trials and temptations that have snared us. All have been soiled by the things they have faced through offense and sin. When the new birth or (born again experience) occurs through the redemptive power of accepting Christ as Lord and Savior all past sin is washed away. This is what Jesus said He must do for us to have a part in Him. If one does sin after that point they must see it as sin and repent to remain a part of Him.

He was bruised, broken, and stained so we can be free.

1 John 1:9

If we confess our sins, He is faithful and just to forgive us our sins and to cleanse us from all unrighteousness.

Chapter 11

His Kingdom Divided

Jesus Had to Do it The Fathers Way

1 Corinthians 11:3 But I want you to know that the head of every man is Christ, the head of woman is man, and the head of Christ is God.

Jesus has a head over Him and <u>its God the Father.</u> The fact is we all have to submit to God's order of authority; God designed it that way for unity.

The church has undergone great turmoil through the greed of man to have power and glory. To give the impression of being more favored by God makes one feel superior. God is no respecter of persons. He only rewards those who are obedient to His voice. This is His kingdom, His power and His glory. We are called to be a functional part of the body of Christ under His authority. We are not called to divide His Kingdom.

Separating His Sheep

I have spoken to so many people who say they've had their fill of God and His church.

The contention of man denies the authority of Christ, man's head. We need to have the same mind as Christ. If we lose sight of Christ, who was completely obedient to God, the result will cause those around us who are trying to comprehend what the kingdom of God is, to once again become scattered back into the world through worthless contention.

Why? Because they will become infected by **<u>the war of lusting to obtain,</u>** which is observing those around them in the church who want to obtain things for their own ideas and glory which will ultimately **cause them to be divided and fall away from Christ**.

Coveting in the church **disrupts Gods household of faith and causes division amongst the congregation.** It's a horrible desire to take over someone's assignment from God. We must seek God for His plans for our lives and the lives of those around us, for His glory. If we should see others fault, it's not to judge them. It's our duty to pray God would correct and restore them for His names sake. **God has His order to restore those in error of His ways through repentance. He also will remove those in rebellion to His Word and refusing to repent.**
(Matthew 18:15-17) (Galatians 6:1)

James 4:1-3 Where do wars and fights come from among you? Do they not come from your desires for pleasure that war in your members? You lust and do not have. You murder and covet and cannot obtain. You fight and war. Yet you do not have because you do not ask. You ask and do not receive, because you ask amiss, that you may spend it on your pleasures.

Chosen and Appointed

John 15:16-17 You did not choose Me, but I chose you and appointed you that you should go and bear fruit, and that your fruit should remain, that whatever you ask the Father in My name He may give you. These things I command you, that you love one another.

God has thought-out our responsibilities in the church. He has equipped His leaders to speak into our lives concerning His way of doing things. Sure many know about God, but **they have to be supplied by God** to do what He is wanting accomplished. We should remember our duty is to fear God always and keep His commandments, and to tell the people the good news that we can have an eternity in heaven because of Jesus Christ.

Ephesians 4:11-13 And He Himself gave some to be apostles, some prophets, some evangelists, and some pastors and teachers, for the equipping of the saints for the work of ministry, for the edifying of the body of Christ, till we all come to the unity of the faith and of the knowledge of the Son of God, to a perfect man, to the measure of the stature of the fullness of Christ;

And He himself has set five separate leadership positions in charge of educating us for the unity of faith. So we can walk in the fullness of Christ in the present time. **He has wonderful plans for each of us** we must be patient and obedient as we learn His ways.

Resisting Gods Authority

Romans 13:1 Therefore whoever resists the authority resists the ordinance of God, and those who resist will bring judgment on themselves.

We have our duties to perform in Christ. The problem is we see people doing this or that and start visualizing how we would do it if it was our duty. Then somehow pride enters in as **we are seeking our own imaginations and confuse it as God speaking to us**. If one could look back at the original point the thoughts started they'd see the pride that started the whole judgment. The Word of God tells us we are to cast imaginations down and not dwell on them.

We all have a longing to serve God, but we must wait for His appointment to service. Zacharias John the Baptist father had to wait for his turn to burn incense in the Lords temple. **(Luke 1: 8-9)**

Disaster came to two hundred fifty impatient priests who God did not choose for service in burning incense. Yet they tried to force their way into Aaron's position with Moses. **(Numbers 16:35)**

No one can just decide what they are going to do in Gods kingdom, He does. It's all in His appointed calling and timing that any duty should try to be preformed.

Prepare your Heart to Seek God

2 Chronicles 12:14 And he did evil, because he did not prepare his heart to seek the LORD.

Cain and Korah did not prepare to seek the Lord they wanted it their way. Cain thought his offering was a good offering, but it wasn't what God had established. Korah and his company thought they should have Moses and Aaron's positions, but weren't called. If they would have set their hearts to do it Gods way their stories would have had different endings.
(Genesis chapter 4, Numbers Chapter16)

In all of our days we need to patiently keep our hearts prepared to seek the one in charge, the Lord. What does His Word say? His thoughts and His ways are higher than ours. If our thoughts are different and we don't prepare ourselves to seek God; we'll then allow our flesh freedom and it will not follow the heart of God.
(Isaiah 55:9)

Galatians 5:13 "For you, brethren, have been called to liberty; only do not use liberty as an opportunity for the flesh, but through love serve one another."

Good Fruit - is Who We Are

Acts 10:38 How God anointed Jesus of Nazareth with the Holy Ghost and with power: who went about doing good and healing all that were oppressed by the devil; for God was with him.

God Himself has also anointed us through the Holy Ghost to do good works. Our anointing is to bring the light of His love to those within our reach to break the oppression of the devil. He has given us His divine nature of life and Godliness to walk in His ways through the power of His word. We need to allow each other do their specific assignment from God. We are to be imitators of Christ full of the Holy Ghost doing good and speaking good words those who are oppressed by the devil.
(Acts 26:18, 2 Peter 1:3-4, 1 John 2: 20, 27)

He Just Wants Us to See Clearly

Romans 12:9-10 Let love be without hypocrisy. Abhor what is evil. Cling to what is good. Be kindly affectionate to one another with brotherly love, in honor giving preference to one another;

In the Lord's Prayer Jesus Himself spoke these words for all who will believe and follow them: **Our Father in heaven, Hallowed be your name, your kingdom come, and your will be done on earth as it is in heaven.** God's Holy Word should direct all of our actions into agreement with Him. His written Word is His mind to us His body of believers. On earth Christ followed Gods Spirit and we are to be led by the same Spirit and **God gets the Glory for being God.** We are His children not hypocrites we follow Him because we know His love and mercy. Daily He reveals the things which try to cause unrighteousness so we can separate ourselves from them.

Mark 7:6-8 He answered and said to them, well did Isaiah prophesy of you hypocrites, as it is written: This people honors Me with their lips, But their heart is far from Me. And in vain they worship Me, Teaching as doctrines the commandments of men. For laying aside the commandment of God, you hold the tradition of men the washing of pitchers and cups, and many other such things you do.

The word hypocrites, interprets stage player or actor. Do want to be a stage player or a child of the Most High God?

Our hearts in the past have been trained with the traditions of men, but God says old thing pass away and all things become new when we accept Christ. Through temptation and a lack of Gods knowledge some have allowed things to enter into the church that even the world knows God does not approve of. Those who have knowledge and maturity need to seek God to restore those who still have faults. If we don't remain gentle with restoration, then we will get caught up and over taken by the temptation ourselves to sin. **(2 Corinthians 5:17) (Galatians 6:1)**

Proverbs 22:4 By humility and the fear of the LORD Are riches and honor and life.

Different experiences in my life have taught me about responding with more humility and fear as I walk with God.

Sound the Alarm

Have you ever repeatedly heard something in your spirit sounding? On this one occasion for several days within my spirit I kept hearing the words, patty cake, patty cake, sound the alarm! My husband had been away and I wasn't able to discuss this with him. I had been greatly disturbed by the message in my spirit. He was on his way home and I just had to go meet him. After his arrival as I went to speak to him and I was compelled to just take my hands like playing patty cake and sound out, I've heard this for three days, patty cake patty cake sound the alarm, patty cake patty cake sound the alarm! I don't know why I let loose then and there it was like a tea pot finally being able to whistle. Later I thought just as the tea pot whistles its alarming ring, God compels us like a whistling tea pot to cry out like John the Baptist and our Lord Jesus declaring, "Repent for the kingdom of heaven is at hand." We are at war. Sound an alarm wake up and remember our cause for Christ and the lost people who are going to hell.

God has placed a burning desire within my soul to be a missionary to the people of my country. This desire has caused me to begin to see the need of sharing the love of Christ publicly, to honor my fellowman who has not yet heard of the love of Christ.

Many I talk to say, they've tried church but, they have stopped going. These are the ones who have fallen away from the church who didn't get to experience Gods fullness before their fall. They need the Word of God reapplied to their desperate hearts. I realized I can't do this alone, so I was humbled and started praying for those chosen by God to also hear the alarm and be moved to speak. Together we must do battle for the souls of those who don't know Christ and Heavens Words of God's love and peace.

We the church must continue to go out in the power of His love, with one purpose to gather His children for the Kingdom of God.

Luke 11:17

But He, knowing their thoughts, said to them: Every kingdom divided against itself is brought to desolation, and a house divided against a house falls.

Chapter 12

His Kingdom is Peace

In Genesis chapter three Adam and Eve ignored Gods instruction and ate the forbidden fruit **the knowledge of good and evil.** Before this Adam **never knew fear**. He had a perfect relationship with His God. So here comes God calling out to him and **Adam ran and hid himself**. Why, because **the peace he had with God had been interrupted.**

Good news! Jesus who successfully lived without ever ignoring God purchased peace back for us.

Peace As the World Gives

John 20:21 So Jesus said to them again, Peace to you! As the Father has sent Me, I also send you.

Jesus speaking here makes a profound statement to His disciples and all who will believe His words. Peace to you!

John 14:27/a Peace I leave with you, My peace I give to you; not as the world gives do I give to you.

<u>Not as the world gives</u> states there is a difference in how peace is administered. The world here is in reference to the men of the earth who are alienated from God and hostile to the cause of Christ and the peace they offer.

James 3:14-18 But if you have bitter envy and self-seeking in your hearts, do not boast and lie against the truth. This wisdom does not descend from above, but is earthly, sensual, and demonic. For where envy and self-seeking exist, confusion and every evil thing are there. But the wisdom that is from above is first pure, <u>then peaceable,</u> gentle, willing to yield, full of mercy and good fruits, without partiality and without

hypocrisy. Now the fruit of righteousness is sown in peace by those who make peace.

The world's peace has its own way of manifestation which doesn't originate from God. **The world's peace comes from self gratification of the mind**. A few examples could be illustrated like this.

1. Someone needs a bill paid and there is no money to pay it. There is an abundance of worry over the situation until there is a solution. **Peace only comes when they think the problem is solved.**

2. Someone has committed an awful deed and they would like to try and cover up their actions. So now they are going to devise a plan to blame someone else. After they had done all they can to point to the other person and believe they have covered their tracks; **they have obtained a temporary peace.**

3. Someone has become offended and they want revenge. They devise a plan to execute revenge and after they have done everything to satisfy their revenge; **there's finally peace, but for how long and at what cost?**

4. Someone may be jealous and by manipulation they cause the person they are jealous over to break all other relationships, **so they can have a sense of peace.** They don't realize that they have no trust or faith in that the other person. The question is now this; just because all other relationships have been temporally severed, does the other person really care for them with their whole heart? Demand and force has its way, but it is not the way of God.

The method people without Christ's Spirit will use to try and obtain peace can be horrifying. Without the Holy Spirit guiding us there really is only a false sense of peace. **Without Gods peace the soul can't have the rest it is longing for.** If God came calling out to a person after they obtained a false sense of peace they would immediately return to fear and hide themselves upon hearing His voice.

The Peace Jesus Left For Us

Godly peace comes from the Holy Spirit. It is a peace that exceeds all understanding. This means things look real bad and no solution is visible, but you can't explain how your heart is guarded from worry and **your mind is free from fear because of His supernatural peace**. **(Philippians 4:6-7)**

The world or those who haven't received Christ can't understand that there is a peace that only comes through the Spirit of God that arises and keeps one at peace while hoping for a solution. **Peace during the middle of a storm is what Jesus left those who believe in Him**. After any one receives Christ into their heart the old way of thinking needs to be replaced with the Word of God. This is the understanding that the world lacks. Without the Holy Spirit inside of an individual no one can understand the gift of peace that only comes from Jesus.

Holy Order Brings Peace

God chose us to be holy people. **Colossians chapter three** deals with the actions we are to put off in order to stop any disturbance that comes to try the soul. God has given us His holy order within the family member to keep peace and unity between each other. **Man over the wife, then they together as parents over the children, and all of them together submits to Gods word**.

Colossians 3:12-15 expresses how important it is to forgive as God forgave us. By acting in mercy and using all the fruit of the Holy Spirit we can choose not to complain against each other.

Colossians 3:12-15 Therefore, as the elect of God, holy and beloved, put on tender mercies, kindness, humility, meekness, longsuffering; bearing with one another, and forgiving one another, if anyone has a complaint against another; even as Christ forgave you, so you also must do. But above all these things put on love, which is the bond of perfection. <u>And let the peace of God rule</u> in your hearts, to which also you were called in one body; and be thankful.

When the peace of God is in place and is ruling in one's heart, it won't allow a disturbance to manifest in the soul. You've heard the saying hold your peace well that's what must be done. We can only hold on or let go of peace. If we do not keep it in place something else will take over that place in us. Peace is having its rule over our life when we can remain with the same way of thinking no matter what tries to invade our thought process,

Philippians 4:6-7 Be anxious for nothing, but in everything by prayer and supplication, with thanksgiving, let your requests be made known to God; and <u>the peace of God, which surpasses all understanding, will guard your hearts and minds through Christ Jesus.</u>

It is our anxiety of the unknown which causes the disturbance that tries to wrestle with our peace.

Isaiah 26:3 <u>You will keep him in perfect peace</u>, whose mind is stayed on You, because he trusts in You.

As one gains knowledge of the Word of God and His peace we realize His administration of peace protects our hearts and minds against the unknown.

Ephesians 6:15 and having <u>shod your feet</u> with the preparation of the gospel of <u>peace</u>.

The ability to love our fellow man during adversity and not walk out of Gods peace, but to be able to stand in His love is part of Gods holy amour that protects our comings and goings in life. We are to dress our feet with His peace and not be lead to our own works which tries to obtain the world's peace. God has a plan we just the need confidence to let Him cover our steps in life. As we just keep holding on to His peace and walk in His love we recognize we now have an ability to overcome fear. It is that wonderful experience of peace that gives us our strength to stay faithfully on Gods course no matter what we have to face in life. It is our hope. **(Romans 5:5)**

Isaiah 55:11-12 So shall My word be that goes forth from My mouth; It shall not return to Me void, But it shall accomplish what I please, And it shall prosper *in* the thing for which I sent it. For you shall go out with joy, <u>and be led out with peace</u>; the mountains and the hills shall break forth into singing before you, and all the trees of the field shall clap their hands. Instead of the thorn shall come up the cypress tree, And instead of the brier shall come up the myrtle tree; and it shall be to the LORD for a name, for an everlasting sign that shall not be cut off.

When he sends His word to a situation we have His peace and joy. His word says to be still, stand, and see the salvation of the Lord. **(Exodus14:13, 2 Chronicles20:17)**

Because we know His Word is true then we are able to trust His plan. Instead of our souls being pierced by the thorn and brier of fear and sorrow, we can have the peace and joy which allows us to clap and sing His praise. Yes, we can rejoice in God instead of walking about in sorrow and fear.

Isaiah 53:4-5 surely He has borne our griefs and carried our sorrows; yet we esteemed Him stricken, Smitten by God, and afflicted. But He was wounded for our transgressions, He was bruised for our iniquities; <u>the chastisement for our peace</u> was upon Him, and by His stripes we are healed.

A situation may rise where panic comes to attack ones mind, but the combination of joy and peace rises within to restore the soul.

Lamentations 3:26 It is good that one should hope and wait quietly for the salvation of the LORD.

God is teaching us to walk through the storms of life holding His peace; it is that peace that rises and keeps us until the trial is over. It is this gift from God's peace that makes the difference through the storms.

God's peace serves our mind and heart as it gently sweeps away fear and doubt. His peace helps us love and not be bitter towards life situations.

His peace also leaves the joy of Lord within us that builds our trust and confidence in His ability.

Peace is not afraid to receive help from the other fruits of the Spirit; Love, Joy, Longsuffering, Gentleness, Goodness, Faith, Meekness, and Temperance. Peace can love when love is not deserved; it has joy and is faithful while waiting on Gods plan. His peace suffers long without complaint because it continually forgives. It's gentle and good by not striking back. His peace helps one to be humble and not wrestle against God's plans. His peace takes hold of ones temper and helps us to remain calm in life's battles.

Peace Comes Forth to Do the Particular Job at Task and Manifests Itself in Many Expressions

Hold your peace	Answer of peace
Extend peace	Peace returns
Give peace	Make peace
Peace be to you	Peace offering
Covenant of peace	Words of peace
Peace on all sides	Shall be peace
Peace and truth	Abundance of peace
Peace and quietness	Sent in peace
Return in peace	To thy grave in peace
Perfect peace	Shall be in peace
Lay down in peace	Speak peace

Sleep in peace	Seek peace
Shall bring peace	Pray for peace
Counselors of peace	Great peace
His government of peace	Way of peace
Ambassadors of peace	Ordain peace
Fruit of the lips-peace	Publishes peace
Led forth with peace	Time of peace
Prince of peace	Life and peace
Peace be within these walls	Peace be still
Righteousness and peace	Chastisement of our peace

Godly Peace Comes From the One Perfect Mind of God

Psalms 85 LORD, You have been favorable to Your land; You have brought back the captivity of Jacob. You have forgiven the iniquity of Your people; You have covered all their sin. Selah You have taken away all Your wrath; You have turned from the fierceness of Your anger. Restore us, O God of our salvation, and cause Your anger toward us to cease. Will You be angry with us forever? Will You prolong Your anger to all generations? Will You not revive us again, That Your people may rejoice in You? Show us Your mercy, LORD, And grant us Your salvation. I will hear what God the LORD will speak, <u>for He will speak peace To His people</u> and to His saints; but let

them not turn back to folly. Surely His salvation is near to those who fear Him that glory may dwell in our land. Mercy and truth have met together; <u>Righteousness and peace have kissed.</u> Truth shall spring out of the earth, and righteousness shall look down from heaven. Yes, the LORD will give what is good; and our land will yield its increase. Righteousness will go before Him, and shall make His footsteps our pathway.

Because of Adams disobedience to God our peace was greatly disturbed. It took several centuries for the peace of God to be restored to mankind through the chastisement of Jesus.
(Isaiah 53:5)

When a storm comes into one's life it builds and moves and has many effects of washing for good and evil. The good that was once in place can be horribly disturbed. Then the evil that rampantly ripped through at one point of the storm can leave its hold as it altars one's behavior. The storm is not over until peace has been restored. We are to cast down imaginations and everything high thing that exalts against the knowledge of God and make all of our thoughts obey the Word of God. **(2Corinthians 10:5)**

Prayer: 1 Thessalonians 5:23 Now may the God of peace Himself sanctify you completely; and may your whole spirit, soul, and body be preserved blameless at the coming of our Lord Jesus Christ. Amen!

Chapter 13

What about Grace

Noah was Found to be Perfect

Genesis 6:8-9 But Noah found grace in the eyes of the LORD. This is the genealogy of Noah. Noah was a just man, perfect in his generations. Noah walked with God.

Noah found grace and walked with God. What more can we say about Noah?

Genesis16:11-13 The earth also was corrupt before God, and the earth was filled with violence. So God looked upon the earth, and indeed it was corrupt; for all flesh had corrupted their way on the earth. And God said to Noah, The end of all flesh has come before Me, for the earth is filled with violence through them; and behold, I will destroy them with the earth.

Noah had no desire to be violent or corrupt; he was found to be just and perfect by God. He had allowed his nature to be affected by God. This nature brought Noah God's grace. Noah was instructed by God to build an ark because God was displeased with the way man had turned to violence and corruption. Because of his obedience he was delivered from God's wrath. What was God's reason in rescuing one man and his family? To show His gracious love for mankind that in the generations to come through Noah's seed others might also be found having no desire for violence or corruption.

Abraham was Commanded to be Perfect

Genesis 12:1-4 Now the LORD had said to Abram: Get out of your country, From your family And from your father's house, To a land that I will show you. I will make you a great nation; I will bless you And make your name great; And you shall be a

blessing. I will bless those who bless you, And I will curse him who curses you; And in you all the families of the earth shall be blessed. So Abram departed as the LORD had spoken to him, and Lot went with him. And Abram was seventy-five years old when he departed from Haran.

Abraham's faith in God is the heart of a holy covenant between God and man. God looked at every nation and all were unusable as far as making one of them a holy before Him. They all had false gods and corrupt ways and were full of violence. So God took one man away from all he knew. Through that man He created a new holy nation unto Himself. God put His ways before him and Abraham followed the way God chose for him to live. Abraham learned God was faithful and he was faithful to his God.

Genesis 17:1-7 When Abram was ninety-nine years old, the LORD appeared to Abram and said to him, I am Almighty God; walk before Me and be blameless. And I will make My covenant between Me and you, and will multiply you exceedingly. Then Abram fell on his face, and God talked with him, saying: As for Me, behold, My covenant is with you, and you shall be a father of many nations. No longer shall your name be called Abram, but your name shall be Abraham; for I have made you a father of many nations. I will make you exceedingly fruitful; and I will make nations of you, and kings shall come from you. And I will establish My covenant between Me and you and your descendants after you in their generations, for an everlasting covenant, to be God to you and your descendants after you.

Galatians 3:29 And if you *are* Christ's, then you are Abraham's seed, and heirs according to the promise.

God called Abraham to make covenant with him and his seed. God chose to make Abraham and his seed a blessed and fruitful nation. When God called Abraham he followed God and taught his seed Isaac to follow God. When we individually are called out by God and by faith follow Him. We become the seed of Abraham by belonging to Jesus and following God therefore part of that holy covenant.

When Abraham was ninety nine God told him, I Am the Almighty God, walk before me and be thou perfect. **(Genesis17:1)**

We have already read Noah was found to be perfect and now God is telling Abraham to be perfect. What does God mean by be perfect?

Walk: to lead, bring, carry, and cause to walk

Perfect: complete, whole, entire, wholesome, unimpaired, innocent, having integrity, and healthful. What is complete or entirely in accord with truth and fact.

Who Ever Believes in Christ Becomes Perfect

When we, like Abraham, believe God is truth we will no longer act upon the rules to this world, but will do our utmost to have our minds renewed through reading the Word of God to establish what is good and acceptable to God. **(Romans12:2)**

Psalms 23:3 He restores my soul; He leads me in the paths of righteousness For His name's sake.

John 1:14-17 And the Word became flesh and dwelt among us, and we beheld His glory, the glory as of the only begotten of

the Father, full of grace and truth. John bore witness of Him and cried out, saying, "This was He of whom I said, He who comes after me is preferred before me, for He was before me. And of His fullness we have all received, and grace for grace. **For the law was given through Moses, but grace and truth came through Jesus Christ.**

John 3:17 For God did not send His Son into the world to condemn the world, but that the world through Him might be saved.

I've been a Christian for years, but even so I mess up daily in one way or the other. There is no excuse for sin. I have come to realize Jesus is the light of the world and His light exposes truth. His Holy Spirit of light and instruction examines sin, righteousness, and judgment. Jesus did not come to condemn, but bring the truth that shows us what sin is. Once sin is revealed as sin, those that follows Gods ways turns and walks away from it, thus is separated from its effects. **(Ephesians 2:8-9)**

No Longer Under the Law but Grace

God really does love the worst sinner and wants to bring all of us to repentance and save us from His eternal judgment. By His grace He sent Jesus to show us how to follow Him. His convicting love shows us what was wrong about our past sinful actions. That's where Jesus the light of the world comes into play; Gods son Jesus came to reveal truth. No one deserves Gods rescue from sin but, His love and grace gave it through Jesus paying the price for our guilt. Our part is accepting what God has provided for us, **Jesus' release from sin.**

Romans chapter seven under the old covenant law they used the example of marriage to explain the covenant between man and woman. Under the old covenant only by death can one released be from their marriage covenant. In other words, one of the covenant members must die before then the other member is released from their covenant agreement.

Redemption: buy back, restoration, saving from corrupted state

Romans 7:1-3 Now, dear brothers and sisters you who are familiar with the law don't you know that the law applies only while a person is living? For example, when a woman marries, the law binds her to her husband as long as he is alive. But if he dies, the laws of marriage no longer apply to her. So while her husband is alive, she would be committing adultery if she married another man. But if her husband dies, she is free from that law and does not commit adultery when she remarries. (New Living Translation)

Next they used the example of Jesus Christ to show how in His death and resurrection the covenants were changed. The son of God died himself and broke **the old covenant which was the law of Moses.** Three days later He rose again to join us to **the new covenant of His grace which is the new law of the Spirit, which is the life of Christ Jesus**.

Romans 7:4 So, my dear brothers and sisters, this is the point: You died to the power of the law when you died with Christ. And now you are united with the one who was raised from the dead. As a result, we can produce a harvest of good deeds for God. When we were controlled by our old nature, sinful desires were at work within us, and the law aroused these evil

**desires that produced a harvest of sinful deeds, resulting in death. But now we have been released from the law, for we died to it and are no longer captive to its power. Now we can serve God, not in the old way of obeying the letter of the law, but in the new way of living in the Spirit.
(New Living Translation)**

When one dies to sin in receiving Jesus the Christ, they pass from the old life of the law of sin and death to the newness of the law of the Spirit in life in Christ to live in the grace of God.

Through one's repentance of sin, Jesus removes the penalty of the law and stops the condemning judgment.

What the law couldn't do grace has done.

If one would sin under the old covenant of the law the penalty was God's wrath and death.

If one would sin under the new covenant of the grace of God the Holy Spirit in love will convict one to repent of sin. Whether or not they submit to the Spirit is discerned by God. Be not deceived sin still has a penalty but grace gives us the power to turn from sin to live in the Spirit of Christ.

Galatians 6:7 Do not be deceived, God is not mocked; for whatever a man sows, that he will also reap.

Romans 2:1 For the law of the Spirit of life in Christ Jesus has made me free from the law of sin and death.

To summarize it all, we who were created by God were once under the law by His covenant to Abraham's and his seed.

In order for a covenant to be broken one must die to break the covenants bond. Then if God who came to earth as the man Jesus Christ died on the cross He broke the old covenant. He still being God established the new covenant of the law of the Spirit in the life of Christ Jesus to anyone who by faith chooses Jesus Christ. When anyone chooses to be bound in a covenant marriage to Christ they are no longer under the Law of Moses. Jesus broke the chains of sin and death and now allows man to be born again by Gods Holy Spirit and be united in a Holy covenant to God despising sin. This is how we become one with Him as they are one in each other.

Father Keep Them Through Your Name

When I asked in prayer for the Lord and Savior Jesus Christ to come and live in me I didn't know the fullness of His love. I just knew I needed a Savior. I recognized His love and experienced His mercy toward my pitiful sinful state. I felt His Spirit come live within me and immediately knew I hated sin. I had so much garbage inside of me. I started to realize by the Word of God there was junk that I needed to get rid of. Just as we clean house, God calls this process sanctification. It was the Word of God which brought this conviction and only the word of God could renew my mind. It is His grace through His Word that has taught me what is what. Decades have passed and I've had my different trials. I've learned to listen to the still small voice of God through the indwelling Holy Spirit which talks within my spirit. It is what has taught me to recognize this world's sin.

James 1:21 Therefore lay aside all filthiness and overflow of wickedness, and receive with meekness the implanted word, which is able to save your souls.

John 17:11 Now I am no longer in the world, but these are in the world, and I come to You. Holy Father, keep through Your name those whom You have given Me, that they may be one as We are.

Jesus prayed that the Father would keep us during our journey here so we can be joined to Him forever in heaven. Through grace we are walking in His goodness and have a godly desire to stop sinning. Why, because the principles have been changed and suddenly we are walking in the all sufficient ways of our God.

God's ultimate grace is just as an earthly father would turn their child in the right direction to go, God turns us towards the light of the world, Jesus; that we might be restored into fellowship with Him.

God is good to the ungrateful and the evil, our proof was Him sending Jesus. Jesus is just waiting for those who want to have a holy relationship with Him. God is still looking for those who hate corruption and violence and will embrace His perfect ways.

God told the Apostle Paul His grace is sufficient, we must learn to walk in His grace. **(2 Corinthians 12:9)**

Tap Into That Grace

Knowing within ourselves Gods grace forgave us our trespasses, we in turn should walk in the same grace toward ourselves and forgive and love ourselves. As we desire to show Gods grace to ourselves will be able to express mercy and grace to others. This is giving grace for grace.

1 Peter1:4-6 Blessed be the God and Father of our Lord Jesus Christ, who according to His abundant mercy has begotten us again to a living hope through the resurrection of Jesus Christ from the dead, to an inheritance incorruptible and undefiled and that does not fade away, reserved in heaven for you, who are kept by the power of God through faith for salvation ready to be revealed in the last time.

We have a heaven waiting for us with no violence or corruption. It's a perfect place for those who will deny ungodliness, worldly lusts, and be sober and righteous before our God in this present world. **(1 Peter 1:4)**

Titus 2:11-13 For the grace of God that brings salvation has appeared to all men, teaching us that, denying ungodliness and worldly lusts, we should live soberly, righteously, and godly in the present age, looking for the blessed hope and glorious appearing of our great God and Savior Jesus Christ,

Hebrews 13:20-21 Now the God of peace, that brought again from the dead our Lord Jesus, that great shepherd of the sheep, through the blood of the everlasting covenant, Make you perfect in every good work to do his will, working in you that which is well pleasing in his sight, through Jesus Christ; to whom be glory forever and ever. Amen. (King James Version)

Chapter 14

His Spirit Is Upon Us

PART ONE

After writing this chapter I feel I must talk some about it before it is read by you. Under the law and before the resurrection of Jesus Christ the Holy Spirit of God was administered differently. Under the law God's Spirit came upon man, but since the out pouring of the Holy Spirit on the day of Pentecost, God's Spirit, if invited will dwell within a man. **(Acts 2:1-4)**

And He Who Trembles at My Word

Isaiah 66:2 for all those things My hand has made, and all those things exist, Says the LORD. But on this one will I look: On him who is poor and of a contrite spirit, and who trembles at My word.

Contrite: repent deeply, sorry for behaving wrongly

Tremble: to shake slightly, continually, uncontrollable with fear, vibrate

Look: direct eyes at, to search with eyes, consider something

God is searching for those who are truly sorry for acting any other way than His. Those who will actually respect His Word and will be obedient to what He says.

I remembered when I started writing my first book, I'd wake up time after time and I'd look at the clock, and it would be 2:59 a.m. and suddenly turn 3:00 a.m. This has been signifying in that I had definite thoughts as I would wake each time and knew they were from God. I had the choice each time to roll back over and go back to sleep or have fellowship with God. So with immediate attention I'd chose to write down the different thoughts, pray in

His Spirit, study His Word, and that is how I wrote my first book. So this morning my thoughts went to two different sets of words. The first set of words were **He anoints my head with oil, (Psalms23:5)** the words of King David.

The Spirit of the Lord Came upon David

1 Samuel 16:13 Then Samuel took the horn of oil and anointed him in the midst of his brothers; and the Spirit of the LORD came upon David from that day forward. So Samuel arose and went to Ramah.

Anoint: to smear, to anoint, consecrate, an inaugural ceremony for the priest

Anointed: consecrated portion

Consecrate: declare place holy, dedicate something to a particular purpose

Why did God have Samuel anoint David's head with oil? God wanted to pour His Spirit on David so he could rule His people His way. When Samuel anointed David's it allowed the Spirit of God to flow into the mind and spirit of God's chosen one.
(1 Samuel 3:20)

David knew the presence of Gods Holy Spirit and had a great desire to follow Gods heart. Though there was a time that David followed His own heart and this caused him to experience a loss of God's holy presence. **(2 Samuel chapter 12)**

With a contrite spirit David cried out to God to return His presence. When Gods Holy Spirit cleansed his heart and restored his soul he knew he was back in a right standing with God. He desired a steadfast spirit that would always discern transgression so he could teach the people Gods ways.

Psalms 51:9-13 Hide Your face from my sins, and blot out all my iniquities. Create in me a clean heart, O God, and renew a steadfast spirit within me. Do not cast me away from Your presence, and do not take Your Holy Spirit from me. Restore to me the joy of Your salvation, and uphold me by Your generous Spirit. Then I will teach transgressors Your ways, and sinners shall be converted to You.

In **2 Samuel 24** David also had a temptation involving his pride. He wanted to count the people to see how powerful his army was. So he instructed Joab the captain of his armies to count Israel and Judah. Well Joab asked David, why do you want to do this thing? Joab knew that God had the power to do the miraculous and make the army a hundred times stronger during battle. Nevertheless Joab obeyed his king and counted the army any way. Joab was trying to show David it wasn't the size of the army that brings the victory; it was that God has to approve whether or not he should go to battle. Judgment came to David, but God showed His mercy because David was honest once he recognized his sinful of pride.

1. When the prophet came and spoke of the abominable thing David did against God in counting the people he didn't make excuses for his prideful decision.

2. When the hand of judgment came on David's kingdom he knew he served a righteous God and just repented.

3. Because David was king this man Araunah offered David his threshing floor and all the sacrificial items for his offering to God at no charge. David refused Araunah's gift and paid him full price

for the items. David knew he couldn't try to offer God something that cost him nothing.

2 Samuel 24:24 Then the king said to Araunah, No, but I will surely buy it from you for a price; nor will I offer burnt offerings to the LORD my God with that which costs me nothing. So David bought the threshing floor and the oxen for fifty shekels of silver.

The Spirit of the Lord Departed

1 Samuel 15:21 But the people took of the plunder, sheep and oxen, the best of the things which should have been utterly destroyed, to sacrifice to the LORD your God in Gilgal.

When the instruction of God came to Saul through the prophet Samuel he didn't obey. Saul had his own idea which taught his kingdom to disobey God. He as king was responsible to make sure those He was ruling followed the same instruction He was given. God wanted the enemy destroyed and never dealt with again, but Saul kept alive the king and the people kept alive the animals.

The prophet Samuel came back with this next Word from God; what's that bleating I hear in my ears? The people assumed God would accept the enemy's sheep and oxen as an offering. While Saul had pride that he captured the king and disregarded the Word of the Lord subsequently it caused Gods Spirit to depart from him and Saul was overcome by distress.

1 Samuel 16:14 But the Spirit of the LORD departed from Saul, and a distressing spirit from the LORD troubled him.

Two Kinds of Hearts

What was the difference between David and Saul? David followed Gods heart and Saul followed his own heart.

When Saul was held in account to God for his disobedience he gave an excuse without repentance. To think our own idea will stand against God's authoritative word is deception. Just because one believes something should happen doesn't mean God is behind that belief. Satan, Cain, and King Saul all fell under pride, because they formed their own ideas instead of obeying God's instruction.

When David was held in account to God for his disobedience he cried for mercy. He asked God to create in him a clean heart then he accepted Gods perfect judgment with a respectful contrite heart.

There is a Spirit Within People

Job 1: 9 Then the LORD said to Satan, Have you considered my servant Job, that there is none like him on the earth, a blameless and upright man, one who fears God and shuns evil?

God orchestrates a test for Job that confirms he has a contrite heart. He loses his children and his fortune and even his body is allowed to be tormented. Being steadfastness Job continues to be blameless and upright before God.

Job 32: 6-13 So Elihu son of Barakel the Buzite said: I am young in years, and you are old; that is why I was fearful, not daring to tell you what I know I thought, Those who are older should speak, for wisdom comes with age. But there is a spirit within people, the breath of the Almighty within them that

makes them intelligent. Sometimes the elders are not wise. Sometimes the aged do not understand justice. So listen to me, and let me tell you what I think. I have waited all this time, listening very carefully to your arguments, listening to you grope for words. I have listened, but not one of you has refuted Job or answered his arguments. (New Living Translation)

Had Job lost his relationship with God? His three friends try to figure out where he went wrong with God, because they had no answer in presumption they spoke, condemnation, surely you must have sinned.

Looking into this scenario we see the fifth man Elihu. Elihu does everything in Gods correct order. He comes, he sits, he attentively waits and listens for words of wisdom from his elders concerning Job's situation. Job speaks as he tries to justify his sinless relationship with God. Then Elihu listens to Eliphaz, Bildad, and Zophar Job's three friends speak as they grope for words with spiritual intelligence. Elihu hears all he can take and can bear no more and even though he's the youngest with this understanding he must speak. Sometimes it's not by age, but by Gods Spirit one is made intelligent. Not one of you can prove Job has done anything wrong or answer his questions about his ruin. <u>Elihu goes on to say Job I advise you not to speak to God in such an attitude. God has a purpose for this trial you're in and opposing Gods methods and not humbling yourself through it will only prolonging the outcome.</u>

Sometimes we aren't wise. Elihu knew wisdom only comes by the breath of God and when that breath speaks into a situation. Elihu had the understanding that Job needed to wait and listen for the Words of the Almighty God. **(Job Chapters 32-36)**

<u>Job realized he had only heard of God before, but when he saw him face to face he cried out I take back everything I said and I sit in this dust to show my repentance. Then God restored twice as much as Job had.</u> **(Job 41:5, 6, 10)**

Through these three men King David, King Saul, and Job we can see that God is sovereign and He alone can discern what's actually has taken place within in a man's spirit.

PART TWO

Luke 1: 13-15 But the angel said to him, Do not be afraid, Zacharias, for your prayer is heard; and your wife Elizabeth will bear you a son, and you shall call his name John. And you will have joy and gladness, and many will rejoice at his birth. For he will be great in the sight of the Lord, and shall drink neither wine nor strong drink. He will also be filled with the Holy Spirit, even from his mother's womb.

God filled John the Baptist with the Holy Spirit inside the womb of his mother Elisabeth. When Mary the mother of Jesus arrived to visit Elisabeth her cousin, the Spirit within Elisabeth's unborn child John leaped, as he bore witness of Jesus the Christ within Mary's womb. **(Luke1:41-44)**

The Spirit Rests Upon Jesus with Power

The second set of words I remembered thinking on this morning were; **(Luke 4:18)** the words Jesus read when he was handed the book of Isaiah. He read **Isaiah 61: 1 The Spirit of the LORD is upon Me, Because He has anointed Me To preach the gospel to the poor; He has sent Me to heal the brokenhearted, To proclaim liberty to the captives And recovery of sight to the blind, To set at liberty those who are oppressed.**

Prior to this event in **Luke 3:21-22 through Luke 4:1-14** talks about Jesus being baptized in water by John and the Holy Spirit descending and resting on him. Then Jesus being full of the Holy Spirit was led to the wilderness to overcome the devil's temptation. Then Jesus returned to Galilee in the power of the Holy Ghost and news quickly spread about Him.

So **Luke 4:18-21** goes on to say how it was customary for Jesus to go to Nazareth and read in the synagogue. He stood up to read and was handed the book which contained the prophecy of **Isaiah 61:1**. When He finished the reading, He closed the book sat down and spoke this day prophecy is fulfilled in your ears. He was proclaiming the power from on high was resting on Him to preach the gospel to the poor. This power would free all those who are captive and restore sight to the spiritually blind. It would ultimately heal the brokenhearted and release those who are oppressed of the devil.

Doing it Just Like the Father

John 5:19 Then Jesus answered and said to them, Most assuredly, I say to you, the Son can do nothing of Himself, but what He sees the Father do; for whatever He does, the Son also does in like manner.

Himself: personal behavior, own action

Jesus carried on each day communicating with the Father so he could behave the same way.

The Promise Came to Those Who Tarried

Isaiah the prophet prophesied about the everlasting covenant of those who would be appointed to be the priest and servants of God in **(Isaiah 61: 6-11)**.

Luke 24:49 Behold, I send the Promise of My Father upon you; but tarry in the city of Jerusalem until you are endued with power from on high.

Acts 1:8 But you shall receive power when the Holy Spirit has come upon you; and you shall be witnesses to Me in Jerusalem, and in all Judea and Samaria, and to the end of the earth.

Acts 2:4 And they were all filled with the Holy Spirit and began to speak with other tongues, as the Spirit gave them utterance.

Tarry: to wait in expectation of something

Endued: to endow somebody with an ability or quality

Jesus told His disciples to wait with expectation to be endued with the Fathers power from on high. **Acts 2:4** records the actual first manifestation of those being filled with the Holy Spirit. The book of Acts includes the records of many other believers in Jesus Christ receiving the power of the Holy Ghost.

Paul and the Holy Spirit

Acts 19:11-12 now God worked unusual miracles by the hands of Paul, so that even handkerchiefs or aprons were brought from his body to the sick, and the diseases left them and the evil spirits went out of them.

As I was reading the book of Acts I noticed the Apostle Paul's followed unusual instructions by the Holy Spirit. Paul was instructed to go to Damascus and he went. **(Acts 9:6)**

When his instructions stated not to go to the towns of Bithynia and Jerusalem he didn't. **(Acts 16:17 and Acts 21:4)**

I recognized Paul's connection with the Spirit of God and the anointing of miraculous power which was produced by his obedience to follow the Spirit.

By Gods grace we as believers have been given special anointed gifts also to supernaturally prophecy, minister, teach, encourage, give, rule, show mercy, love, and show kindness. **(Romans 12:6-10)**

1John 2:27 but the anointing which you have received from Him abides in you, and you do not need that anyone teach you; but as the same anointing teaches you concerning all things, and is true, and is not a lie, and just as it has taught you, you will abide in Him.

Try the Spirits

God warns us in the last days there would be many false prophets and we are not to believe every spirit, but to try them all.
(2 Peter1:1-3) (1 John chapter 4)

Not everyone who says they are proclaiming Gods word is following His Holy Spirit. The book of **Jude** states many have crept into the church and are spoiling the things of God. Jude says they are sensual not having the Holy Spirit. He tells us to keep our selves built up in love and to pray in the Holy Spirit looking to Jesus for God's mercy.

Jude 1:21 but you, beloved, building yourselves up on your most holy faith, praying in the Holy Spirit keep yourselves in the love of God, looking for the mercy of our Lord Jesus Christ unto eternal life.

Studying the book of Jude has caused me to repent of my harshness and judgment of other believers. It has opened my eyes to the self pride and arrogance that tries to creep into ones heart which ultimately tries rule others with an unholy spirit. God wouldn't tolerate it in those Jude used as examples and He won't tolerate it in us either. The part that really spoke to me was verse nine the wisdom of Michael the arch angel. He knew not to even rail against the devil, but said the Lord rebuke you. In conclusion we must always try the spirits and like Jude truly discern what God regards as His Holy Spirit within us.

Chapter 15
Understanding Temptation

Proverbs 14:12 and 16:25

There is a way

That Seems Right

To a Man

But it's End

Is the Way of Death

Temptation

James 1:13-15 Let no one say when he is tempted, I am tempted by God; for God cannot be tempted by evil, nor does He Himself tempt anyone.

In **Matthew 4:4, 8, 10** Jesus uses three responses to His temptation.
#1 Man shall not live by bread alone, but by every word that proceeds from the mouth of God.
#2 You shall not tempt the LORD your God
#3 You shall worship the LORD your God and Him only you shall serve

I have been taught of the Holy Spirit and the Word of God to pay attention to the emotions that stir with in me. Fear, anger, pride, or just being dissatisfied tells me something is wrong in my Spirit. Seconds count when any temptation tries to arise. Note! These emotions are trying to carry offense deep into the heart.

James 1: 14-15 But each one is tempted when he is drawn away by his own desires and enticed. Then, when desire has conceived, it gives birth to sin; and sin, when it is full-grown, brings forth death.

Desire: to take pleasure in, delight in, be pleased to do, ask for, beg

Temptation makes one desire things that are ungodly. Ungodliness is driven by lust or an intense desire to take pleasure in something Gods says is unholy. If the promptings by the Holy Spirit are ignored through enticement of one's own desires verses Gods Word; lust could have full rule. Lust if given opportunity and the

Holy Spirit is ignored, will cause spiritual blindness. Lust has nothing to do with love. Lust is unclean and love is holy.

Genesis 4:6-8 so the LORD said to Cain, Why are you angry? And why has your countenance fallen? If you do well, will you not be accepted? And if you do not do well, sin lies at the door. And its desire *is* for you, but you should rule over it. Now Cain talked with Abel his brother; and it came to pass, when they were in the field, that Cain rose up against Abel his brother and killed him.

Cain knew what God required for an offering. Abel respected God and Cain didn't. God had observed Cain's temptation to sin. God instructed him to go do well and to rule over sins Temptation. Cain allowed the sin to rule him and it resulted in his brother Ables death.

The Apostle Paul warned the believers that these are perilous times full of envy, pride, and every deceptive evil work that tries the heart of man. Sin is trying to rule over the hearts of man. Many things from Gods Word will be exposed in this chapter. I pray that you will receive a blessing from it. **(2 Timothy 3-6)**

Wallowing: roll in something, indulge in something excessively, condition of depravity, and walk with difficulty

Romans 5:21 so that as sin reigned in death, even so grace might reign through righteousness to eternal life through Jesus Christ our Lord.

Because of temptation all have sinned and come short of His glory. Everyone must understand there's a penalty of death for sin. <u>**The death penalty for sin can be reversed**</u> if one repents of their sins and allows Christ to remove it.

Romans 6:23 For the wages of sin *is* death, but the gift of God *is* eternal life in Christ Jesus our Lord.

We must learn to turn from the world's darkness and embrace His way of light. **(Acts 26:18)**

Sometimes it takes awhile to recognize what ones flesh had been wallowing in. Sins pleasure excites the flesh and makes one spiritually blind. I myself have in the past blindly allowed self pity and bitterness to rule within my soul. All of the sudden I became conscious of what I had been wallowing in and my soul longed to be cleansed and refreshed by the Word of God. God restored my soul once I confessed it as sin and turned back toward His Word.

He restores my soul and He leads me in paths of righteousness for His names sake. (Psalms23:3)

Psalms 37:4 Delight yourself also in the LORD And He shall give you the desires of your heart.

Delight: enjoyment, pleasure, happiness

A Simple Dream

Once I had a dream that changed the way I looked at offense and its effects. In this dream I was sitting on a wall overlooking the street. All of a sudden a team of horses came wildly rushing out of control through the street and then out of sight. I started speaking with different people in the dream. One at a time they told me stories of things that suddenly entered their lives that brought

horrible offense. Each situation was similar in that just like those horses coming and rushing through suddenly they had no way to control their circumstance. Not one of them knew what to do. They were allowing the circumstances to take its course lacking Godly wisdom to remove the offense. Then we discuss their present life conditions. In each situation we considered the consequence of not letting go of the offense. As we spoke they gained the understanding that they had been led into captivity by their grudges and they learned that holding a grudge brings condemnation and Gods judgment and they must forgive to be forgiven.
(Matthew 6:14-15) (James 5:9)

What was so neat about this dream was; I could relay God's way to each person teaching how offense is the thing that tries to separate us from God's way of life and that offense is what causes one to walk in the flesh. If offense has its full rule ultimately it may cost them their inheritance in Gods kingdom. They each had to decide how to go on would they hold on to the offense or would they let it go?
As I left each person I felt my heart was truly full of gladness. As I took one last glance at each person's expression and noticed each one had a great big smile, because they received the knowledge of God's Word without offense. Then I woke up with a smile on my face and gladness in my heart.

His Kingdom His Power and His Glory

I really get frustrated with all the things I have no control over yet they continue to stare me in the face. I'm so expressive, just ask anyone who's had opportunity to see me in action. Picture me standing in front of my husband hysterically crying. I have no power! I have no power! What do you think my husband did in all of his wisdom? He just looked at me and stared, never said a word. So then I exclaimed this is God's kingdom and His power, I have no power to get anyone to do anything! Well I guess I felt better, because I just went to my room and cried. However, God knew something; I finally realized He has all the power and I only thought I did. He is the one that makes things happen. After I resurfaced my husband said, what are you trying to make me do now? I looked at him and said nothing I was just realizing God has all the power and I turned and walked away.

There have been times I'd try to get someone to do something and they just ignored me. Here's an example for years I have tried to get this one thing accomplished, but all my efforts couldn't get my husband to budge. When someone has knowledge or strength that you don't have and they don't help it's hard not to hold a grudge.

This is how I conquered holding the grudge and letting God deal with it in His time. One day I asked my husband for help with something I couldn't do and I had waited six years to get it completed. I walked away and said, God I won't hate him if he doesn't help me. I choose to love him anyway. I'm sorry for the grudge I've had over this. No sooner I said that, he said go get this and that. What I had waited six years for was completed in about an hour. I'd suddenly realized when any one responds to me, God is doing what I can't. We tend to think if I was the one with the strength and knowledge I'd respond and help. So when others don't respond this makes us feel we have a right to hold a grudge. I realized not everyone is like me and truthfully I don't respond to everything others want me to do either.

I've thought how offense comes just like that team of horses out of control. With no one controlling it, offense is almost an unstoppable force.

Jesus defeated offense and its temptation as he resisted it through the Word of God.

The Apostle Paul cried out to God when tempted to be offended and God responded His grace is sufficient.

2 Corinthians 12:9 And He said to me, My grace is sufficient for you, for My strength is made perfect in weakness. Therefore most gladly I will rather boast in my infirmities, that the power of Christ may rest upon me.

We can trust in God's power that lives within us. God knows the beginning of a trial and its end. It is His power when we are weak and are battling offense that He shows itself strong. He is the way, the truth, and the life. His grace is sufficient. It is enough. He considers the entire matter in all matters, because He is the beginning and the end. His Holy Spirit judge's between sin and righteousness and the only power we have in any matter is to learn to fear God and keep His commandments. **(Revelations1:8)**

Ecclesiastes 12: 13-14 Let us hear the conclusion of the whole matter: Fear God and keep His commandment, for this is man's all. For God will bring every work into judgment, including every secret thing, whether good or evil.

If you would like to ask Jesus to come into your life and be your Lord and Savior say this simple prayer.

Dear Jesus I realize all have gone their own way. I realize I have committed my own sins. Please wash my sins away. Make me a new person in your mercy and grace. Forgive my trespasses in life and help me to be born to your ways in this life. Jesus, I ask this in your holy name. Amen

If you prayed that prayer and would like to write me:

Jesus and Jami

P.O. Box 854

Hannibal, MO 63401

You can purchase copies at:

www.jesusandjami.com

and Amazon.com

Made in the USA
Columbia, SC
29 April 2018